ANNIE HEPPENSTALL

SEARCH ME
AND KNOW ME

ANNIE HEPPENSTALL

SEARCH ME
AND KNOW ME

Spiritual Accompaniment through
Reflection on the Celtic Cross

**kevin
mayhew**

kevin mayhew

First published in Great Britain in 2015 by Kevin Mayhew Ltd
Buxhall, Stowmarket, Suffolk IP14 3BW
Tel: +44 (0) 1449 737978 Fax: +44 (0) 1449 737834
E-mail: info@kevinmayhew.com

www.kevinmayhew.com

9 8 7 6 5 4 3 2 1 0

ISBN 978 1 84867 764 7
Catalogue No. 1501467

Cover design by Rob Mortonson
© Images used under licence from Shutterstock Inc.
Edited by Nicki Copeland
Typeset by Julie Francis

Printed and bound in Great Britain

Contents

About the author   6

Acknowledgements   7

Introduction: How to use the book   9

Part 1: Who am I?

Chapter 1   Perspectives on the Celtic cross:
a foundational self-reflection   17

Chapter 2   The cross, the tree of life and
our inner being   35

Chapter 3   Human archetypes: the story of our lives   49

Part 2: Where am I?

Chapter 4   Finding our bearings   73

Chapter 5   Inner landscapes and thinness   95

Chapter 6   Being in difficult places: the 'desert'   117

Part 3: Who is with me?

Chapter 7   Soul friends and networks of love   133

Chapter 8   Connecting with creation   183

Chapter 9   Creatures from knotwork   199

Part 4: What time is it?

Chapter 10   Cycles and holy hours   223

Chapter 11   Moon months   237

Chapter 12   The solar year and its relationship
with the liturgical year   245

Part 5: What have we done?

Chapter 13   The Celtic cross, the elements
and human impact   257

Chapter 14   Conclusion   279

About the author

Annie Heppenstall is a qualified teacher and has a degree in Theology and Religious Studies from Cambridge University. Trained in spiritual direction and counselling skills, she applies her experience and interests in writing, leading workshops and retreats and supporting others in different ways in their own spiritual journeys. Among other things, Annie is a professed Franciscan Tertiary, drawn to expressions of earth spirituality and expressions of the feminine divine. She lives in a richly multi-faith area of the Midlands with her husband and son.

For details of other books by Annie Heppenstall published by Kevin Mayhew, please refer to our website: www.kevinmayhew.com

Acknowledgements

Search Me and Know Me would not have been written without the practical, emotional and spiritual support of my husband and dearest soul friend, Ray Gaston: thank you, Ray!

I would also like to thank all the people involved in the process of putting this book together, including those who, through diverse encounters over the years, have inspired the journal examples and helped me to clarify the 'inclinations' in the first chapter. I have written all journal examples in a way that should make it impossible to identify anybody personally. I would like to say a special thank you to Revd Julian Francis and the folk of St George's Church, Edgbaston, for all their interest and kindness in inviting me to lead a very enjoyable parish weekend at Cropthorne during the formative stages of the book, and to Daphne Cook and Helen Woodall, for such supportive conversation and friendship as the book took shape.

To Ray and Luke with love

Introduction

O Lord,[1] you have searched me and known me.
You know when I sit down and when I rise up;
you discern my thoughts from far away.
You search out my path and my lying down,
and are acquainted with all my ways.

Psalm 139:1-3

Search Me and Know Me is a workbook for self-exploration, using the symbol of the Celtic cross as a primary framework. It offers a variety of opportunities to consider personal perspective, experience and response to life lived as spiritual journey. Psalm 139, quoted above, expresses awe at God's complete knowledge of us and our ways, which is more complete than our knowledge of ourselves.

As we go through life we gradually learn more about ourselves. Although we can see ourselves very critically, and can be influenced by the way we believe other people see us, we also have the potential to look deep within at the bare bones, so to speak. Self-understanding can become a path to self-acceptance and self-forgiveness as we learn to have compassion on ourselves – even as we are assured that God has compassion on us. This can begin a profound journey towards inner peace and healing, and in turn can open up our capacity to try to understand and have compassion on others.

No prior knowledge of or involvement with 'Celtic' Christianity is necessary to use this book. I use the word 'Celtic' with caution: while I rarely use inverted commas around

---

1. Quotations from the Bible are all from the NRSV which follows the convention of replacing the holy name of God (Exodus 3:14) with 'LORD', rendered as 'Lord' in this book. In my own writing, I avoid ascribing a gender to God.

the term beyond this passage, it is important to appreciate that it refers primarily to a language group (Welsh, Irish, Scottish Gaelic, Cornish, Breton) rather than a distinct cultural or racial group, and that what is popularly seen today as a creation-friendly and 'alternative' approach to Christianity is a modern phenomenon with diverse expressions, drawing inspiration from rather than reproducing elements of an earlier and complex time period. What is commonly understood as the Celtic Christian period is mainly located in the British Isles and spans a period from the fourth or fifth to the seventh century and longer in Ireland. During this time there were also Christians following the Roman Church tradition – even while married to 'Celtic' Christians – and there were also people resident in the region who did not speak the Celtic languages – such as Anglo Saxons.

While the book is for anybody, it is especially intended for those already established on a spiritual path with an interest in weaving life and faith together with self-understanding; it assumes a belief in God, or a spiritual rather than materialist way of looking at the world. The material and choice of language comes from the Christian tradition. I hope it is accessible to a wide spectrum of Christians across the denominations, as well as to seekers, earth spirituality and Celtic practitioners who do not necessarily identify as Christian. The emphasis is very much on supporting you the reader in exploring your perspective rather than mine, although my general position inevitably shines through. To me, a contemporary 'Celtic' approach to spirituality is full of potential, with its affinity with creation, its connection with the spiritual practice of the Desert Fathers and Mothers, and its strong tradition of poetry, artwork and legend, but also a concern with social justice and ecology. All this combines to offer challenge and inspiration for creativity, alongside spiritual depth embedded in the real world, as we seek fresh directions in down-to-earth spiritual journeying for today.

While aspects of Celtic Christianity lend themselves to a rural setting with all the joys and challenges of proximity to the natural world, the tradition is also appropriate in an urban context. It is very relevant to today's world, in all its complexity and diversity, and can be an approach that supports anybody in their spiritual journey, whatever their background. Although many of us (myself included) now live in towns and cities, and need a spiritual path that can help us make sense of urban life, we also need help keeping our connections open to creation and the wider picture of what humanity is and has been through the ages.

Search Me and Know Me draws on contemporary ideas about how we can help ourselves and one another through increased self-awareness, moving towards the realisation of our full and true potential, in order to live a more fulfilled – and ultimately more loving – life. Modern psychology approaches this work through secular routes, but for those on a spiritual path, the idea of realising true potential is also about uncovering the true 'us', that is known to God, who sees our heart (1 Samuel 16:7) or our true nature.

In the Gospels we are presented with Jesus, who – especially in John's Gospel – has complete self-understanding of his oneness with God. There is an invitation in Christian living to have the same mind as Christ (Philippians 2:5), to think, feel and be like Jesus. This includes or is born from personal realisation of our identity in God, our potential to discover the oneness of which the mystical Jesus of John's Gospel speaks: 'On that day you will know that I am in my Father, and you in me, and I in you' (John 14:20). John's Gospel was beloved of the saints in the Celtic tradition; this quest for oneness with God reverberates through the centuries and connects us with the same desire among spiritual seekers around the world.

In the Celtic Christian tradition which developed in Celtic-speaking regions, those on a spiritual path sought out a soul friend, an *anamchara*, to listen with warmth and wisdom, so communicating the love of God. This book cannot replace a real flesh-and-blood *anamchara*, but it offers companionship in exploring life's journey and in reflecting on that journey and its meaning to us. Personal perspective is explored through a variety of reflections, and the book illustrates ideas with the voices of many different individuals, each expressing their own unique way of seeing things.

'Celtic', it has to be said, is sometimes muddled up with a kind of tribalism, as though it is only for people who claim a particular place of origin. While my own sense of connection with the history, nature and people of the British Isles and Brittany is a very real part of my own background and spirituality, my interest is in increasing global interconnection and mutual respect. My hope is that people with connections and heritage from all around the world can find some point of connection and conversation here – indeed, that they can make a creative contribution that enriches spiritual exploration for all of us as we deepen our understanding of love.

Work through the book as slowly as you like, as an exercise in listening to yourself, taking the time to consider how you feel, what and who you resonate with, and what you are looking for. Then the process can be repeated or referred back to any number of times, because, of course, we change. Depending on your preferences as you work through the book, different prayers, exercises and reflections will speak to you more than others. You will be prompted to keep a journal as you go along, which will gradually build up into a custom-built spiritual resource that suits you for the time being. Throughout the book, there are journaling examples expressing a variety of voices. Whether you find yourself concurring or wildly disagreeing, you can take as much or as little notice of them as you like.

You may have the feeling, when you finish the book, that you are not the same as when you started out, that you have moved on, so the first journal entries exploring your identity no longer quite fit. That is part of the process. Welcome the change, be ready to let go of things you said even days or weeks ago. Don't delete what you wrote earlier – value it, but do not feel constrained by it. You are not bound to any statement of identity longer than you want to be. At the end, you will be able to look back on the whole journey as an expression of who you are in your own wholeness, wholeness which is not a fixed thing, but a flowing, moving, growing entity, on the way to the sea, always the same river but never the same water,[2] from one moment to the next.

Getting started: working alone or with others

If you want to get started straight away, just begin by making notes in the margins of the book, but try to transfer as soon as you can to a form of journaling that works for you. That might be a special notebook or a computer file, or even an audio file if you prefer to talk instead of write. Taking the trouble to keep your thoughts together in a form you can review is part of valuing your own inner feelings and will be helpful later. You can work at this alone, with a spiritual accompanier or as part of a small, mutually supportive group, covering the material week by week.

It can be interesting and thought-provoking to hear others' thoughts as we work out our own, and this is one of the advantages of working in a group or sharing with a friend.

---

2. From a saying attributed to Heraclitus of Ephesus.

Part 1
Who am I?

Chapter 1
Perspectives on the Celtic cross: a foundational self-reflection

This introductory activity is a starting point for the work to come. Make a note of your responses so that you can refer back later.

Find a Celtic cross to look at, such as the illustration on the facing page, or draw a simple one on a piece of paper, made up of a circle and cross. Look at the whole shape of the Celtic cross. If anything, what seems to stand out? Without thinking too hard about it, do you feel most drawn to . . .

- the circle or the cross?
- the centre or the circumference of the circle?
- the horizontal line of the arms (across), or the vertical (up and down)?

Note your initial impulses, then have a look at the interpretation suggestions below, which might reflect something of the kind of language and images you gravitate towards. You may, of course, find more resonance with some of the alternatives, or you may want to completely contradict the suggestions, all of which is fine!

Suggested interpretations

Circle: interest in the cyclical nature of things; continuity; a sense of perpetual motion, wheels turning or the eternal; keywords may include renewal, rebirth, regeneration, return, pattern, dying and rising, sphere, globe, global, whole, holistic, spiral; also valuing daily practice, ritual or routine.

Cross: interest in the linear; the progression from past to present to future; the importance of specific events in the past and future; ideas of beginnings; origins; developments; irreversible changes; decisions and endings; paths reaching into the distance; setting off into the unknown; direction; choices; life as a river.

Centre of circle: interest in the interior life, inner thoughts and feelings; seeking to understand oneself, love oneself, forgive oneself; intuitions; the 'inner being'; contemplation; quietness; concentration; focus; attention to detail; the Divine within; some may see it as 'introversion'.

Circumference of circle: interest in 'out there'; community, the world; engagement with others; activity and concerns in daily life; outreach; welcome; perhaps boundaries; defining group identity; belonging; togetherness; working for the good of the whole; some may see it as 'extroversion'.

Horizontal line: interest in the reality of here and now; the importance of life on earth; the insights we can gain from observation of the world and reflection on history; 'reality' concerns about justice; ecology; peace; the economy; equality; the sense of humanity and/or the natural world as the place of encounter with the Divine; incarnational spirituality; God among us; God present in creation, revealed in creation, only known through creation.

Vertical line: interest in connecting heaven and earth, the physical and spiritual; the journey of the soul from this life to the next, an interest in the beyond; a need to feel a spiritual connection with the Divine, through heightened experiences such as beautiful music or architecture; dreams, meditation, mystical prayer or experiences of synchronicity; a sense of mystery, of 'something other', beyond us; the Divine as transcendent; perhaps an occasional need to escape 'reality'.

Combining the options

The Celtic cross, of course, holds together all these attitudes and more; you may identify with any number of descriptions or want to add to them. The composite descriptions below draw together impressions from the eight combinations that can be made from choosing from the options:

- circle or cross
- centre or circumference
- vertical or horizontal

In combination they may suggest tendencies and preferences in our approach to life, which can help us to understand ourselves at the same time as appreciating that others see things very differently. I have called these eight possibilities 'inclinations'. They are not clearly defined character types and I make no presumption to compete with the Enneagram or Myers Briggs!

Below is a chart suggesting pictorial symbols for each concept, allowing an imaginary scene to form, with scope for personal preference. In keeping with a book about spiritual journeying, exploring the way we can use the Celtic cross to locate ourselves in time and place, the suggested pictures are of imaginary locations or environments which might attract us.

We are, of course, all different, and our outlook shifts and changes as we go through life, so it is not surprising if we find ourselves moving between the descriptors and forming our own, based on our unique perspectives on life, or finding that they do not quite fit. If you found it difficult to make your mind up about choosing between any of the pairs in the Celtic cross reflection, circle/cross, centre/ circumference, vertical/horizontal, then read each of the descriptions that could have been possible choices and decide for yourself which you prefer. It may also be of interest to read the 'opposite' inclination and see whether it also speaks to you – for example if you chose centre, circle, horizontal, the opposite would be circumference, cross, vertical.

The correspondence of symbols is as follows:

Celtic cross	Interpretation	Symbol
cross	linear	road or river
circle	cyclical	sun or moon
centre	inner	cave or hut
circumference	outer	village – a cluster of huts
vertical	heights and depths	tree or mountain
horizontal	here and now	sea or lake

The eight inclinations

1. Circle, centre, horizontal

Imagine a cave by the seashore in the light of the sun (or variations using the chart above, such as a hut by a lake in moonlight).

This combination suggests an inclination towards solitude and the contemplative life. Time and space for reflection and self-understanding are important, represented by the solitary cave or hut and the presence of the lake or sea. Insight and peace of mind come from noticing changing moods, patterns and relationships of the earth, sea and skies and of living things, and how they relate to the whole and to the individual. Through patient observation, one might develop the ability to anticipate patterns, recognising the appropriateness of time and season, often with an intuitive grasp of what is timely or below the surface or a wish to explore more deeply. The Divine is located within, in others, in life itself and in all creation.

Feelings and being able to go with the flow are important, likewise the freedom to practise personal routines and rituals. Individuals drawn to this combination may well seek to develop qualities of love, gentleness, peace and so on, in order to extend these outwards into the world, and may be self-critical of less admirable traits. They might identify loosely with groups and prefer to avoid labels and constraints. Others may be frustrated by an apparent unpredictability or changeableness, which can unintentionally come across as being aloof or distant.

Hope is found in expressions of regeneration and reassurance of a new dawn or the coming of springtime, at times perhaps a little idealistically.

The combination suggests someone who may feel frustration with superficiality but, conversely, may prefer to keep things light and on the surface, perhaps out of a reluctance to engage with the more challenging depths. This contrast is represented by the surface of the water in the picture: some sail on the surface; others dive down below the surface – and others, like a diving bird, do both.

There may be a tendency to retreat into solitude during times of difficulty rather than reaching out for companionship, and this can lead to feelings of isolation. Such times come and go, and the self-aware individual recognises passing phases for what they are and makes peace with the ebb and flow of life.

2. Circle, circumference, horizontal

Imagine a village by a lake, in the sunlight (or variations such as a village by the seashore).

This combination suggests an inclination towards community life and immediate experience of the world and its natural cycles, and a concern for maintaining natural processes and the welfare of others, especially dependents. Daily routines and seasonal activity may be part of this interest, including an enjoyment of celebrating special festivals marking key points in the year as a family or group and seeing these as times for special generosity and regard for others. Insight comes from noticing patterns and relationships, especially between people and how they relate to the whole. Hope lies in the idea of a spiritual network of love and self-giving that connects all, like a web, in ever widening circles. Challenge comes in the form of disruption to routines and from those who do not want to join in; it can be tempting to judge the more introverted as antisocial.

Belonging and making a contribution to community are important; the Divine is located in loving community, and creation is especially appreciated for the abundance of the earth in supporting life – as represented in the lake full of fish. There is a need to be grateful, to manage and take care of the earth for the sake of future generations. This requires skill and knowledge, so respect is due to those who can instruct the community wisely, drawing on genuine practical experience. Much shared effort revolves around provision for the well-being of loved ones, of the whole and of future generations. Particular concerns arise when nature is seen to work 'against' humanity: creativity goes into finding ways to reduce the risk of natural disaster or to enhance the effects of nature, such as producing a higher crop yield or harnessing solar energy.

There is a real desire to create loving relationships within the group, so that all appreciate the interdependence and mutual accountability. This can sometimes manifest as a tendency towards the accidental formation of cliques or even a degree of tribalism which makes it difficult for outsiders to join, unless they are ready to assume the group identity and blend in. The flip side of this loving bond is a mistrust of those outside the group and a tendency towards negative stereotyping. There is not a great deal of time for introspection in this picture, which can result in difficulty in seeing one's own unconscious expectation that others must conform to the pattern in order to belong, but there can also be a high degree of generosity, warmth and willingness to extend hospitality.

3. Circle, centre, vertical

Imagine a cave on a mountainside in the moonlight (or variations such as a hut beside a tree in the sunshine – or even a shelter within a large, hollow tree).

This combination suggests an inclination towards the interplay between the cyclical nature of creation, the importance of pattern and routine or ritual and the experience of the transcendent breaking through. There may be a concern for the human calling to link 'heaven and earth', and an awareness of human failure in this respect – the need to experience the Divine within, mystically and personally. This approach can involve the need to find a higher or deeper meaning to a situation, a need to feel spiritually connected, to experience the present moment intensely yet with a sense of mystery, that there is more to reality than meets the eye. Hope lies in the quest for deeper insight, in flashes of inspiration and sudden feelings of being very 'alive' and connected to all that is. These can be times of great creativity, which are balanced by times of searching for a truth or an insight that is just beyond reach. Time and space for retreat, study or contemplative solitude – time to think – is important, represented by the cave or hut. Developing creative skills is also important, so that these insights can be communicated to others.

Frustrations can include the interruption of personal reflection or focus by the demands of everyday life, which can seem irrelevant to what really matters and result in impatience with what is perceived to be meaningless, mundane or shallow. The meaningful, however, is approached with passion and dedication, like a strong tree growing up into the light, a blessing to many.

There may be a strong sense of individuality, which may appear to others as an unshakeable confidence, perhaps stubbornness, the mark of a leader or person of great insight. There may be a freedom to speak one's mind and an ability to express what others dare not or cannot articulate, whether through humour or superior knowledge or insight, which demands a degree of respect, whether the individual is liked or disliked. Although they may be highly personable, such a person does not change through coercion or peer pressure but only in their own time, having drawn their own conclusions about the 'truth'.

4. Circle, circumference, vertical

Imagine a village nestled in the foothills of a mountain, in the sunlight (or variations such as a village with a tall tree at the centre).

This combination suggests an inclination towards the interplay between the cyclical nature of creation and the experience of the transcendent breaking through, a concern for the human calling to link 'heaven and earth', and an awareness of human failure in this respect – the need to experience the Divine in community and to support or work with others in bringing about transformation. This approach can involve a hunger to find spiritual meaning through work and engagement with others, and can accompany a feeling of great compassion for others and a desire to communicate or give something of worth to them, even an insight into Christ among us, often selflessly. Hope lies in the love and positive responses experienced through reaching out to others.

The tendency is towards the importance of love in action, the bringing down of heaven to earth or the lifting up of the mundane to sanctify it, through prayer and praise. Communal worship and shared prayer may be important – the shared experience of the Spirit, and of lifting local and global concerns up to God together, experiencing the joy and strength of unity as a people dedicated to Christ. There may also be concerns about how God's people should behave, issues of morality and clear ideas of what brings God's blessing or constitutes a sin or a falling away from God. This can lead to feelings of disappointment with others, a desire to keep people together or a fear of judgement, as well as strong hopes in a heavenly reconciliation or reward, and the importance of ideas of salvation. At a personal level, it can lead to a constraining or hiding of behaviour because of majority values and ideas about God, which can create feelings of inner conflict.

The picture suggests a settlement which is quite self-sufficient, as though living in a bubble, or one's own little world – a microcosm of the macrocosm, where the minutiae of daily life is what absorbs care and attention and the outside world has less impact. This is represented by the absence of a road in the picture – as though visitors are rare, coming on foot in small numbers and receiving special attention, whether welcoming or hostile. The absence of a road also implies that this village is difficult to leave and can become claustrophobic, even though in other ways it feels very safe.

5. Cross, centre, horizontal

Imagine a cave on the seashore, with a path running along the clifftop (or variations such as a hut between a lake and a road).

This combination suggests a strong sense of the significance of past and future, of being on the way towards something unknown but important – as represented by the path – but also a need for interior peace of mind in the present moment, as represented by the cave. This is a place of refuge or retreat, a safe space in which to free oneself from qualms about the past or anxiety about the future, by concentrating on the present and what is to be gained by living well. There is a strong willingness or desire to work on personal development to understand oneself better and avoid making the same mistakes again, or to gain wisdom from past experience which will inform future choices. There is also a sense of the importance of this world, of the planet and population's future, and a concern with attitudes and work that will heal or improve the situation for everybody.

This desire for self-development can prompt one to seek out teachers, whether acknowledged as such or not, who will have an influence for a while – before one moves on again. This hunger for guides and teachers can lead to disillusionment, through setting people up on pedestals which they eventually fall off – until one learns to accept that nobody is perfect.

The 'cave' is likely to be seen as a temporary shelter rather than a permanent dwelling – journey is important. Such a person may appear as something of an itinerant, a traveller on the way, possibly not fully appreciating or engaging with others in their own right but as a means to further their own progress or personal vision. On the other hand, such people can be capable of great love which is free of attachment or possessiveness, able to delight in an encounter in the present moment and move on, feeling blessed and giving blessing, without strings attached.

The location by the sea or lake represents something of the sense of the infinite or the vastness of the Divine breaking through into the present. The path, which is a vital and exciting (or perhaps frightening) lifeline to the world, can also be represented by a boat voyage over the sea, supported by the mysterious water and empowered by the wind of the Holy Spirit. The call to new adventures, new experiences of what it is to be alive, are difficult to ignore, despite the protestations of the more settled.

6. Cross, circumference, horizontal

Imagine a village built on a crossroads by a lake (or variations, such as a village by the sea).

This combination suggests the importance of settlement – a village formed around a crossroads, perhaps a marketplace or other meeting place for councils, exchange, learning and culture – secular as well as spiritual life. Crossroads are important points on the journey, where decisions need to be made and options weighed up, when faced with a choice of possibilities. There is likely to be a strong sense of the significance of past and future, of the potential for exploration beyond this place, of movement towards something unknown and of journeying together – a shared pilgrimage, a convoy, an army even, joining together for companionship as well as the safety and power of numbers. There may be a shared excitement about the way God works with creative potential in humanity; there may also be an inclination to be proactive in gaining and wielding power within society, led by aspirations to make a positive difference, to protect, to defend, even to win new ground.

Responsible leadership and discernment of direction is important – a need to weigh up options, a sense of realism in what is achievable. There is a sense of the importance of this world, of the planet and population's future, and a concern to establish justice and stability. The road is important as a way for people to move on and to link up with other communities, to build alliances and common understandings, to unite against shared threats to peace. This networking is part of the wider vision for the future and the sense of history or identity of the community.

The picture is rather like that of a traditional fishing village where everyone is involved in the shared effort of catching, processing, trading and eating food. It is a thriving network of activity which works best when everybody is on good terms, willing to share challenges as well as celebrations – but knows their place.

There may be a tendency to weigh others up in terms of a transaction – what do they bring to offer? What do they want to take away? What contribution do they make to the whole? There may be little time for those who just want to sit and watch for a while, or who need some space, some time out. There can be a tendency towards heroics, sweeping up and rescuing apparently needy people, as part of the daily work, and a feeling of confusion when such magnanimous gestures seem unappreciated or backfire. There is a sense of the importance of busyness, of outreach, of personal responsibility, loyalty, choice and empowerment. There is a great deal of energy and motivation to do good in this inclination. The challenge comes when others dispute what is 'good' or appropriate action.

7. Cross, centre, vertical

Imagine a cave beside a mountain stream (or variations such as a hut beside a tree and a crossroads).

This combination suggests an inclination towards living on the edge, outside society but loosely connected. There is a link with others – a road or a river – so people can come in their ones and twos to seek this individual out or come across him or her by chance. In turn, the one drawn to this lifestyle can easily come and go, although they may well like to have a home where they feel at peace. There is an inclination towards mysticism, for time out to reflect and be quiet, but this solitude is often used not simply to find peace in the present moment but also for inner journeying, driven by a desire to make progress on the spiritual path.

The sense of linear development is strong. Learning from the past, reflecting on roots and formative experiences, weaves into a concern with aspirations and feelings of true potential, seeking ever greater connection with the Divine, especially through transcendent experience. This could be represented by the presence of a large tree – perhaps an oak, with strong roots and wide, sun-seeking canopy, with the potential of a new tree encapsulated in every acorn that falls.

The importance of life journey is represented in the river, which is constantly flowing on to become one with the sea – an image of union with God. Following this way may become one of personal transformation, with a desire that one may gain spiritual qualities which will be of use to the world – or just to the few who happen to cross one's path. There may be an element of seeking or claiming direct inspiration from the Divine, whether through the words of Scripture or in other ways, and potential for conflict when others challenge the veracity of such convictions or the methods used to develop them. There may also be a pull towards new spiritual experiences encountered by means of the road, river or crossroads – for example from other traditions, which may puzzle or perturb others. The desire to encounter the Divine outweighs the pressure to conform to a tradition, although the sense of rootedness or belonging remains important: this may at times be a source of inner conflict.

8. Cross, circumference, vertical

Imagine a village on the banks of a river, with a tall tree or trees (or variations such as a village beside a mountain stream).

This combination suggests inclination towards dedicated spiritual community with a sense of the significance of shared human journey, moving together towards a greater sense of connection to the Divine, especially through transcendent experience. This approach may involve working with others in supporting transformation of the community or the wider world, with a desire that the divine presence will be known on earth and that people will gain a sense of 'salvation' or of the Holy Spirit at work.

The symbol of the river is important, and represents the presence of the Holy Spirit in community, sustaining the lives of the people and providing the means and energy for moving on. The emphasis is on creating an enthused community that can transform people's lives, not least through intercession, and thus transform the world, bringing heaven to earth. Works of compassion are valuable. Emphasis may be on vocational study and also on understanding the Scriptures, developing prayer life and creating experiences which help people to find God in their lives and thus live to their full potential, with devotion and self-discipline. Community rituals may be valued as vehicles for living life in God's love: rituals of healing, penitence, absolution, initiation and communion as well as life events of marriage and death.

This approach may involve a belief that everybody needs to share the same vision or common understanding or dedicate themselves to the same 'rule', rather like a rowing crew all needing to pull together, or a ship's crew that is united in a common aim to stay afloat and reach a destination.

This can mean that conflicts and concerns occur when differences of opinion arise, or challenges to authority or refusal to recognise established authority.

The picture reflects something of the vision in Revelation, of the river of life with trees of healing along its banks, with leaves and fruit for the well-being of all: an aspiration for spiritual gifts to touch the earth with goodness.

Journaling

Take time to note down your responses to the Celtic cross – the descriptions, pictures and inclinations. This whole exercise is foundational to much that follows.

The comments by other voices, below, are provided as journaling examples. If you find that you prefer not to bother with other people's thoughts, by all means just pass over this section.

Journaling examples

I chose circle, centre, vertical. This is about right. I do tend to notice the cyclical, and like the idea of being able to anticipate what's coming next according to a pattern – spring following winter and so on – whereas I find the idea of an unknown future quite scary. I am very drawn to meditation and silent prayer, and am quite introspective, although I'm not sure I'd use the word 'introvert'. I love people and company, but my spirituality is a rather interior process. The vertical line, for me, is about the spiritual connection I sometimes feel when I am at peace, or deep in prayer, or sometimes in a really beautiful natural place. This is very important: it's part of knowing that the spiritual life is real, that there is a love beyond us that reaches 'down' to us, and I'm sure this only gets better when we die. I do care about life in the here and now, of course I do. The vertical line is quite strong, too; I make an effort to contribute to society – the outer circle – but I have to say the interior, experiential nature of my own spirituality spoke loudest.

Or

I chose cross, circumference, horizontal. I do think a lot about the past and I am always making plans for the future, whether it's a holiday or a community event. I have some trust about the future – it's in God's hands, like I am, and I just keep going along the way as best I can. I am strongly motivated to work for and with the community; I love social gatherings and shared worship; I love singing with others and the satisfaction of working together on projects that actually make a difference. This connects with the horizontal line: I always need to know the latest news and what it means for real people, people we should be supporting with our prayers and whom we might be able to help. I do some voluntary work in the church café, serving and listening to people, and I get as much out of this as the church service – it seems to be the same thing sometimes.

A closing prayer-chant suitable for learning by heart

Holy One and Holy Three,
my whole you know,
my whole you see,
my whole you love eternally,
so let me ever thankful be.
Amen

Chapter 2
The cross, the tree of life and our inner being

*Out of the ground the Lord God made to grow every tree
that is pleasant to the sight and good for food,
the tree of life also in the midst of the garden,
and the tree of the knowledge of good and evil.*

Genesis 2:9

The cross, a simplification of the human form with arms outstretched, was made from a tree. The vertical beam of the cross is derived from the trunk of a tree growing up from the ground towards the sky, and the horizontal beam reflects the branches reaching out to the sides. The cross is poetically referred to as a tree, and in some circles of Christian tradition, the tree of life mentioned in Genesis is interpreted as representing humanity in our pure form, prior to the Fall, while the tree of the knowledge of good and evil is associated with our hunger to know more than is good for us, our temptation to push beyond the parameters that would keep us innocent. This hunger, it is said, is what has made us the way we are – beautiful yet broken, full of potential yet flawed, projecting our complex nature onto the rest of creation and shaping it, both for good and for ill. Either way, we can see the essence of humanity expressed as a tree, whether a tree of knowledge or a tree of life.

By extension, Christ as the perfect human being, fully human yet fully divine, also has a strong association with the tree of life. The cross, too, has been linked in Christian tradition to the tree of life: Christ's work an undoing of the consequences of our predilection for the fruit of the tree of knowledge.

The importance of trees cannot be overestimated. We know now that the very air we breathe is the out-breath of primeval forests. Cultures all around the world hold trees in high regard, often seeing them as a bridge or channel between the three realms of sky, earth and underworld. In Celtic-speaking cultures, it seems that oak trees were especially important; there are many stories of saints who were associated with oaks. St Brigid's Monastery at Kildare was in an oak forest ('Kildare' means Church of the Oaks); St Columba of Iona spoke of how much he yearned for the oaks of Ireland.

But there were also saints who saw the groves as threatening to the Christian faith and confronted local pagans of the day by felling venerated trees as though there could be only one expression of a bridge between the heavens and the earth: Jesus Christ. Yet, all the same, Scripture supports the imagery of the tree in defining our true identity.

A worshipper visiting the temple in Jerusalem declares:

> But I am like a green olive tree
> in the house of God.
> I trust in the steadfast love of God
> for ever and ever.

Psalm 52:8

While King Nebuchadnezzar in his pride dreams of himself as a mighty tree sustaining all the world:

Upon my bed this is what I saw;
there was a tree at the centre of the earth,
and its height was great.
The tree grew great and strong,
its top reached to heaven, and it was visible
to the ends of the whole earth.
Its foliage was beautiful,
its fruit abundant,
and it provided food for all.
The animals of the field found shade under it,
the birds of the air nested in its branches,
and from it all living beings were fed.

Daniel 4:10-12

According to Luke's Gospel, Jesus seems to refer to himself as a tree, or perhaps to felled timber in a carpenter's drying yard, as he journeys towards his execution: 'For if they do this when the wood is green, what will happen when it is dry?' (Luke 23:31). On a different occasion he offers a simple way of discerning who to trust and who to avoid:

'Beware of false prophets, who come to you in sheep's clothing but inwardly are ravenous wolves. You will know them by their fruits. Are grapes gathered from thorns, or figs from thistles? In the same way, every good tree bears good fruit, but the bad tree bears bad fruit. A good tree cannot bear bad fruit, nor can a bad tree bear good fruit.'

Matthew 7:15-18

One property of trees in particular seems to be alluded to by the writer of Ephesians, who talks about being 'rooted and grounded in love', like a tree with roots deep in sustaining, supporting soil:

> For this reason I bow my knees before the Father, from whom every family in heaven and on earth takes its name. I pray that, according to the riches of his glory, he may grant that you may be strengthened in your inner being with power through his Spirit, and that Christ may dwell in your hearts through faith, as you are being rooted and grounded in love. I pray that you may have the power to comprehend, with all the saints, what is the breadth and length and height and depth, and to know the love of Christ that surpasses knowledge, so that you may be filled with all the fullness of God.

> *Ephesians 3:14-19*

This passage in a sense tells us all we need to know about our identity, from a Christian perspective: we are all offspring of one loving God. In the day-to-day experience of life, this big picture sometimes recedes as we see the details of our immediate relationships; what we do; our qualifications and work; our attitudes, skills, preferences and passions; the state of our finances; the homes we live in and so on. We are many things to many people, and these all relate to who we are. But the passage from Ephesians suggests a core 'us', our 'inner being' (Ephesians 3:16, above) – in some cultures symbolised by the heart or belly and in others by the skeleton itself or just the head – that simply exists to love and be loved by God. The writer of Ephesians talks of this essential inner part of us using the imagery of a tree, as being 'rooted and grounded in love'.

A tree grows naturally towards the sun – that age-old symbol of the Divine – and in growing, gains strength (Ephesians 3:15). We might say that our life journey is simply that process of growing towards the light. But if only our lives were so straightforward! If only we had a clear and constant sense of where God is in our lives, then we might grow from the little acorn of our potential, as tall and upright as a solitary oak or the tree of life itself, accepting no other authority, no other influence in the direction of our development.

Some of the Celtic saints, whom we will consider later on, give the impression that they have been people of unwavering faith who have indeed grown up since infancy directly towards God. But most of us are not saints, and life is rarely as easy as that. And besides, if we were to grow up with such unwavering directness, might it not make us a little rigid, a little unsympathetic to the difficulties of others? The twists and bends in the tree trunks of our lives are part of our uniqueness, our individuality; they are testimony to the great search we have undertaken, the great struggle to work out where God is in our lives, every day.

Pruning is a necessary part of the care of fruit trees, and we, too, are pruned as we grow up, by our parents, teachers, communities, society itself. But in learning to adapt to the requirements that society places on us, we can lose touch with what is the real 'us'. The culture in which we grow can shape us a little too much, and we can find, as adults, that we have forgotten who we are. Getting in touch with that sense of 'this is the real me' – our core, which God has never lost sight of – can help us to realign ourselves to our true vision and sense of purpose. Discovering the true light in our lives, and the search for our true identity in relation to God and to the rest of creation, is a significant element of our life journey.

St Brigid of Kildare was one such character who was in touch with her 'inner being' from her earliest days, consistently 'rooted and grounded' in love all her life. There are many stories about the way the child Brigid would give anything away for the sake of helping another in need, human or otherwise. On one occasion she was cooking a meal for her father, the druid Dubthach, and his guests, when a hungry dog appeared at the door. She gave one of the pieces of meat to the dog, risking a scolding, but by the time the meal came to be served the missing piece had miraculously reappeared. When she was in charge of the dairy, she would give away a large percentage of the produce to the poor, yet the supplies of milk and butter never seemed to be depleted. Then there was the time she waited in her father's wagon while he visited the king of the region. Dubthach was hoping to sell Brigid because her generosity was too expensive to sustain, but while he was gone, she gave away his prized sword to a passing stranger! The king made a suitably noble comment about her worthiness, but declined to take her off her father.

Another child might eventually have been intimidated into behaving as her elders wished, and buried their natural generosity under layers of fear and resentment. But neither Dubthach nor anybody else managed to curtail Brigid's childhood compulsion to be generous, and it persisted into adulthood.

It has been said that Brigid's compassion came from God, and this was what made her a saint. Strands of Celtic Christianity tend towards a relatively positive view of human potential, as though we still hold a glimmer of that tree of life within us, broken though we may be. Take the Celtic theologian Pelagius, for example, or Morgan, by his Celtic name. Pelagius said that God's image is reflected in the face of a newborn baby. He taught the importance of personal responsibility for behaviour, in contrast with his more powerful contemporary, Augustine of Hippo, who championed the concept of original sin and the abject condition of humanity in need of Christ's saving sacrifice. Although popular in some circles, in Rome as well as the Celtic-speaking lands, Pelagius lost the debate with Augustine and his name has been associated with heresy (a heresy which is arguably a misrepresentation of Pelagius' actual position) ever since.

There is room in the Celtic tradition to allow for good fruit to grow naturally from a person's heart, and this gives us room to pause and consider what we ourselves think about our own true nature, our inner being and our relationship to God, to one another and to the earth.

A body meditation

The upright Celtic cross, planted firmly in the ground, has been seen as tree-like. Its root plunges into the earth while the trunk ascends skywards, the traditional direction of heaven. Standing upright, we have the same posture, our feet on the ground and the crown of our heads exposed to sun, wind and rain. We, too, as we reflected earlier in the book, are meeting points of 'heaven' and earth.

Stand or sit upright with your hands by your sides, if possible with your feet on the ground. Imagine yourself as a tree, the life-giving rays of the sun shining down on you and the rain falling at your roots, to make you grow tall and strong.

Slowly raise your arms out as the branches of the tree, lifting leaves towards the light. Your leaves breathe oxygen into the world, your branches provide shelter for other living things and, in season, bear blossom then fruit. You are a beautiful part of creation.

Now focus on your heart area, which roughly corresponds to the centre of the cross, and imagine or feel life and love radiating out from you, an energy which flows from you because of the energy you receive from earth and heaven. This is the circle of the Celtic cross spreading out from you like a ripple on the surface of a pond. What is it that you wish to send out to the world today? Is it love? Gentleness? Joy? Peace?

Journaling

Make a note of any thoughts, especially about:

- the tree of life
- the body meditation above
- trees in general
- how you interpret Ephesians 3:14-19, our 'inner being'
- the root of St Brigid's generosity
- the different outlooks of Pelagius and St Augustine (find out more if it interests you!).

42

To what extent do you feel that your own identity is bound up with work, relationships, groups that you belong to and so on?

How might you finish the statement, 'I am a . . .?'

A creative activity for self-reflection

This reflection explores the connection between ourselves and the 'tree', or the vertical axis of the cross.

Sketch a fair-sized tree with roots. Label the trunk 'Me' and label the roots with the names of people who influenced your upbringing. What was your early environment like, that your 'roots' grew in? Label this too. Add branches, and label these with the roles and relationships of your life. If some roles or relationships have ended, you can represent these as branches that have fallen or been cut off, if this makes sense to your life tree. Otherwise leave them, if they continue to be a part of your identity. Sometimes one thing leads to another as new shoots grow from older branches.

Draw some leaves and write down what gives you energy or nourishment to live life as fully as you can, from coffee with neighbours to running marathons.

What are the 'fruits', the good gifts you give to the world? Some of these will be associated with relationships, some with work (the way we spend our time, not necessarily paid).

How do you choose to represent more difficult experiences and relationships? Broken branches? Undeveloped or rotten fruit?

What feelings are you aware of as you draw your diagram?

When you feel that you have finished, stop and review your picture. It expresses something of your wholeness, the 'you' that has stretched from childhood to now, and reflects how you have interacted with your environment and been shaped by it. As you work on your tree, ask yourself how you want to express God's presence in your life, if at all – for example, as sap flowing through the tree, the sun up above or the nurturing earth holding you. In the future, you might want to draw your tree very differently, but what does your tree say to you now? If you feel so inspired, consider turning your diagram into a fuller work of art.

It might be of interest to compare your notes and your drawing with your response to the perspectives on the Celtic cross in chapter 1, especially concerning the vertical beam of the cross.

Journaling examples

I am a . . . daughter, sister, cousin, aunt, expectant mother, wife, graduate, physiotherapist, qualified first aider, house-group co-leader, dog-walker, gardener, dish-washer, laundry-washer, cook, organiser, brunette, busybody, know-all, lapsed guitar player, Myers Briggs ISTJ, in debt . . . All of these are part of me being me!

I drew some big roots: my parents gave me a strong, secure beginning and my family meant a lot to me. My early environment was a safe, quiet, middling kind of neighbourhood where nothing very exciting ever happened. People knew each other; there was the odd dodgy character but nothing too threatening. I was quite well behaved – there wasn't much to rebel against. If anything, I was a bit bored until I went away to university. This was important, my first 'branching out'. I drew some fruit because it helped me get my job in which I help lots of people, but I wasn't sure how to draw the loan I've still not quite paid off – I wanted to draw caterpillars eating the leaves. I had to do the Myers Briggs personality test to get the job so it clearly meant something to my employers, if not to me! I was a bit negative, calling myself a 'busybody' and a 'know-all': the first is from my auntie, who used to tease me for being nosy, and the second is from people at school who resented me doing well. But I worked hard so I deserved it.

I quite like my tree, looking at it makes me realise there are so many dimensions to my life. How will I draw my baby? Will he/she be a really big fruit or what?!

Or

My tree has weak roots. I drew them all scraggy as though they couldn't hold the tree up, and they are in a dump of a place. The roots are sending this message up the trunk that's just mean – not enough water is getting up, not enough love. The tree's all scraggy as though it's growing in a desert. It's amazing that it's grown at all. It's got some branches; some of them are broken. I've drawn some on the ground: my last job, my last partner . . . But how do I draw my daughter – she is one of the real joys of my life. She's still connected to me even though her mum isn't. I've shown her as a little tree growing next to me. I got over alcohol dependency – that's a fruit. What nourishes me? Music.

I look at my tree. Do I hate it? No, actually, I feel sorry for it. I might even be a bit proud of it. I think it's struggling in a difficult place – there's not enough water and the sun's too strong. God's put me in this desert place and is beating down on me, but why? Or maybe God looked down and saw me struggling and shone on me to give me a direction to grow in. I'm here, aren't I? I'm asking about God; I'm not dead yet. I'd really like to have a nice branch with some flowers on.

What can I do? I need some rain, some love, some deeper roots, to go back and find out something about my folks. Grandad. He loved me. The Grandad-memory root can send me up some water, enough to grow a few more leaves. What did he teach me? He used to hold my hand and walk in the park with me, take time to listen to me chattering away. He never said a word to put me down. He listened and his listening was kind. I hope I can be like that for my daughter.

Closing prayer

Loving God, you made me and you love me.
You know my past and you know the pattern of
my potential,
the shape of my life to come,
the choices open to me,
the challenges facing me,
the lessons shaping me,
the joys and sorrows affecting me.

You know my whole, while I see only a part;
you know how I began,
where my roots are planted,
the quality of the soil in which I grow,
you know what dreams and hopes and fears
grew in my heart, from my earliest days.
You know what it is to be me,
and what it is that drives me, inspires me,
excites me, delights me.
So let me know myself as you know me;
let me remember my deepest desire.
Let me awaken to your call;
let me live this unique life you gave me
with all my love and all my strength,
forever nourished by your greater love,
forever growing towards the sun that is you.
Amen

Chapter 3
Human archetypes: the story of our lives

When I look at your heavens, the work of your fingers,
the moon and the stars that you have established;
what are human beings that you are mindful of them,
mortals that you care for them?
Yet you have made them a little lower than God,
and crowned them with glory and honour.
You have given them dominion over the works of your hands;
you have put all things under their feet,
all sheep and oxen,
and also the beasts of the field,
the birds of the air, and the fish of the sea,
whatever passes along the paths of the seas.
O Lord, our Sovereign,
how majestic is your name in all the earth!

Psalm 8:3-9

We are undertaking a reflection on our life journey, and in so doing, we look to our past, our present and the possibilities open to us in the future. Going back to the initial reflection on personal perspectives on the Celtic cross (chapter 1), this focus on the linear passage of time relates especially to the horizontal beam of the cross, the importance of earthly life, the emphasis on what shapes us but which is now gone, and on the unknown which lies ahead of us, in which we encounter many, many different characters and engage in many situations, in a variety of environments that interweave with incredible complexity.

As we progress through our lives, we are naturally shaped by the people and experiences along the way, and we in turn influence others. We, too, have a presence on earth; we occupy a particular place, have a particular perspective on life and a degree of power to change things. Like our life stories as they unfold, we are unique, yet we also have certain characteristics in common with others who are alive now and others who have gone before us. We consider our sense of identity in relation to others.

Since we are especially concerned with how the Celtic tradition can help us to reflect on our own lives, we will spend a little while considering some characters from Celtic legend who might mirror some of our own situations and characteristics. There are some real characters in the accounts handed down to us from Celtic Christian tradition: 'real' in the sense that most of them did indeed exist, although their stories have often been tweaked in the storytelling process, and 'characters' in the sense that they have a kind of storybook quality. There are character types among the personalities, which we might go so far as to call archetypes. We will consider some of the named personalities themselves later on.

The term 'archetype' was explored especially by Carl Jung and has had a great impact on contemporary ways of understanding individuality in relation to the wider experience of humanity. It describes a kind of perfect form, a transcultural, recognisable type. Well-known archetypes include the 'hermit' or 'sage': an elderly man or woman with a staff, cloak and lantern, and perhaps an animal companion, who lives alone and may seem cantankerous at first, but is very wise and usually also very compassionate or very powerful – or both. Another popular archetype is the 'fool': a wanderer, often a youth, who is free of commitments, has the minimum of possessions and attachments, and follows his or her spontaneous inclinations with a kind of naivety that is sometimes irresponsible and sometimes unconsciously profound, often showing a love of song and dance, and a lack of interest in money. Then there is the 'trickster': a loner who is very cunning, and tends to act unilaterally for their own amusement, sometimes causing mischief and sometimes helping people in need, but never predictable, always somewhat challenging, someone to treat with caution.

Archetypes form the skeleton of many a film and novel, especially pantomime, and we first get to know them in childhood, through fairy stories, with human and animal characters. They help children to feel safe with the pattern of the story. But archetypes do not just exist out there in the world of story; they also exist within us and resonate at a deep level because we recognise something real about ourselves and the story of our lives.

It goes without saying that archetypes are not independent, living, spiritual entities attempting to control us; the term is simply a way of understanding the many dimensions of our own complex, unique personalities and roles in life. We often have more than one archetypal character at play at a time, depending whether we are at work, at home or on holiday. Looking back into our past we may notice them in particular people we knew. Reflecting on our response to archetypes can tell us a good deal about what is at our heart, and thus why we respond to the world in the way we do. If I am feeling rather drawn to the idea of the hermit, for example, I am not necessarily in the best frame of mind to think about chairing meetings. If I am

enchanted by the image of a penniless free-spirit wanderer –
a 'fool' – no wonder I feel frustrated if everything and
everyone round me seems to be demanding that I wear my
'responsible householder' hat (and vice versa!).

We cannot always change our circumstances very easily,
but having an awareness of our inner archetypes can help us
at least to understand ourselves a little better, and then to be
gentle with ourselves and even find some humour.

Some types or archetypes that frequent the stories of the
Celtic saints include wise abbots and abbesses, hermits,
wandering preachers called *perigrinati*, adventurers setting
off over the sea in coracles to see where the Spirit would lead
them, independent-minded women who chose monastic life
and an education with the possibility of promotion rather
than marriage (it tended to be either/or in those days), men
and women of mysterious power, from a time when 'the old
ways' and Christianity were rubbing shoulders. These
characters, although coming from a different world in many
ways, still resonate with us and offer us insights into our
own selves.

Below, then, are eight roles that can be found in the
stories of people from the early days of the Christian faith in
the British Isles and Brittany. Read the following
descriptions and pick a character that attracts you or
resonates with you in some way. As you read, you may well
want to make a connection with the eight inclinations
derived from the perspectives on the Celtic cross reflection in
chapter 1. At the end of this chapter I suggest a loose
association between the human archetypes and the
inclinations, but read this after you have formed your own
impressions, not before!

Hermit

Many of the Celtic saints were hermits for at least part of their lives. It was a practice developed by the Desert Fathers and Mothers of the Mediterranean region stretching north from Egypt to Syria. These holy people left the cities, especially Constantinople (now Istanbul) when Christianity became the institutional religion, to seek austerity, humility and the challenge of a natural environment in which to live lives of prayer and soul searching. Groups sometimes formed around these hermits, of people hoping to learn from their wisdom and to find peace through the discipline of a simple pattern of daily living. These communities were the forerunners of early monasteries.

Today, it is unusual and difficult to be able to go 'off grid' and live undisturbed in nature, although some do achieve this. It is also relatively unusual for spiritual seekers today to enter monastic communities – yet, again, of course, some do. Many more of us tune into the pull of the hermit life by taking time for retreat, by creating a quiet corner for ourselves, by joining a community of people who seem to share some of our own spiritual aspirations, perhaps with a 'rule' or pattern of daily life or a time of shared prayer – even across time zones via the internet.

Such people might be drawn to solitude and remote places to be alone with God in nature – or just to be alone with nature. They prefer a simple life, which may seem overly austere to some, and to let creation teach them wisdom about self-sufficiency, mending, recycling, humility, patience, endurance, peace . . . Sometimes one might indeed feel deep peace, but sometimes inner demons surface, which disturb and which need to be wrestled with in prayer. Sometimes the natural world is full of beauty; sometimes it is a hostile environment. Both need to be accepted.

Someone living such a lifestyle may find that others are drawn to them as though by a gravitational pull, but a sign of true wisdom is the refusal to be put on a pedestal by others. Remaining down to earth may be expressed in a special affinity with creatures, or with plants and the soil.

Wandering evangelist or *perigrinati*

Some Celtic saints, men and women, are described as setting out from their homes or monasteries, often later in life having developed a mature spiritual practice, to travel to distant places. The motivation was often to make Christ known through preaching, teaching and example, and often to set up new centres of prayer and worship. This departure from the home community often meant an element of self-denial or sacrifice – the risks of travel and the time it took to travel long distances meant that return could never be taken for granted. At times, leaving a beloved place was forced upon individuals – such as Columba's exile from Ireland following a battle – and had a penitential element, with an aspiration to do as much good as the harm done.

It was common in earlier times to travel by water rather than trekking mile upon mile over forested or marshy ground. Coracles often feature in the stories of Celtic saints, being lightweight basket-like crafts of woven hazel rods or slats covered with waterproofed animal hide. Larger craft, the curragh, were made for sea going, as in the famous voyage of Brendan, which we shall think about later on.

Today, travel is easier and quicker and usually safer – yet still, departure from loved ones and from loved places is a 'big' thing to do and is not undertaken lightly; it can be a 'little death', a 'going west'. Some love to travel, and they go easily; for others it is a terrible challenge, yet when the motive or the sense of 'mission' is strong enough, we find ourselves making the most surprising plans. A traveller might go for all kinds of reasons, but especially, as someone aware of the spirituality of their life journey, to learn more of God and God's world, to experience love and to share love, whether walking or using transport, by talking to fellow travellers and those met along the way. Through meeting all kinds of people, receiving their hospitality with gratitude, supporting them in their labours and standing alongside them in hardships, life is enriched in immeasurable ways. How often do we hear that a 'missionary' discovers, in time, that they have received more than they set out to give, and has learned more than they set out to teach?

Abbot or abbess

Celtic Christianity revolved around monastic communities rather than cathedrals or parish churches, which developed during the Saxon era (possibly according to feudal divisions of land on which local lords built their own chapels and churches and picked their own priests). The monastery often housed both men and women, in separate buildings, and was a centre of local employment, agriculture, learning, care of the sick and shelter in time of need, as well as a focus of prayer. Some, such as Whitby Abbey, under Hilda, whom we will think about later, became centres of excellence, their abbots or abbesses held in high regard. These were often members of the nobility who had chosen a spiritual rather than a secular life, but had found prominence nevertheless. Being an abbess or other leading figure in a convent or monastery was a particularly good opportunity for women to gain respect in their own right.

Today, communities are served by different professions: teachers in schools and colleges, nurses and doctors in hospitals, and employment opportunities vary according to locality. The many roles held together by a monastery have dispersed into a mainly secular society, so most finding themselves at work in the community will not be under the umbrella of the Church, although their motives for a chosen occupation may well be spiritual. Those who find themselves without work, or in work that they do not find satisfying, may hold on to visions of something that is more fulfilling, more useful, more about engaging with real people. What our hearts long for, the communities we'd love to serve and be part of, often relate to our spiritual values.

This archetype represents somebody who is giving of their best for the sake of community. It may reflect a wise and educated leader or co-leader of a community, a teacher, mentor, administrator, guide and/or manager, or a care-giver in a therapeutic capacity. It could also be somebody who is working in a less noticeable position, of equal – or greater – value to the whole. Such a 'servant of the people' may well be sustained by prayer and a love of Scripture, with the needs of others at heart and with qualities of patience, gentleness and discernment.

Anamchara

As we will consider later on, it was thought essential for those following a religious life to have a 'soul friend' or *anamchara*, with whom they could share their deepest thoughts. There are accounts of very strong bonds, relationships of beautiful compassion and devotion often involving one travelling significant distances to reach the other. A soul friend might be a mature member of a monastic community, even someone who had previously acted as a foster parent, as in the case of the Abbess Ita who was a wise soul friend to her foster son Brendan.

Today, we still need soul friends, and we gravitate towards those we find particularly wise and good at listening. We each have our own needs so we are drawn to different people for different reasons, but we have our own ways of knowing who to trust, who is 'genuine', who is living their life in a way that somehow speaks to us.

If we find ourselves in the situation of being a trusted soul friend to another, we know it is a great privilege, but also one which asks qualities of us that we cannot plan or generate for ourselves. We cannot make ourselves wise, or make ourselves humble, although we can learn to be better listeners. So if we know that we have been entrusted with the confidence of another, it is as though we have been handed something precious to cherish and support, and we need to draw on our own relationship with God to be the person the other needs us to be.

A soul friend will sometimes still make sacrifices to be alongside another, listening to them, discussing faith matters, praying with them and communicating Christ's love, and putting their own agenda aside. They will recognise the struggles that others go through to find what they need in life; empathy flows naturally as a gift. Through this loving listening, God sometimes works as a guide, a healer of souls and a comforter, to give challenge and to accompany others through life's joys and pains, even to a person's first or final breath, for the role can be something akin to a midwife to the soul.

Sacred poet

In Celtic cultures, the bard was held in high regard. While some stayed put in a community that could support them in return for their gifts, many travelled a circuit, bringing news and entertainment to the people with song, riddle, poetry and story. They held the people's history, their memory. They could raise a leader up by singing their praises, and they could ruin a reputation, destroy someone's hold on power, through negative portrayals and the art of satire. They were clever wordsmiths and bringers of musical enchantment, beloved but at the same time treated with great respect.

Today, the skills of the bard are dispersed in many ways, from singer–songwriters to satirists, storytellers to film-makers, journalists to archivists. There are those of us who enjoy making music or writing poetry and the like for our own satisfaction, or for a wider audience. The bardic spirit of communication lives, too, in the work of artists who communicate in other ways – through picture, theatre, dance and so much more. Human beings have a vast capacity to be creative and to express themselves, to immortalise important moments in symbolic ways.

As we grow up, our creativity is sometimes encouraged, sometimes suppressed, and finding the 'inner bard' is not always easy. But it is the part of us that is inspired to respond to the world around us, from the depths of our humanity, because our hearts have been stirred and we wish to stir the hearts of others. Those in whom the sacred gift of creativity is strong feel most fully alive when taken by the strange flow of inspiration. The effects of divine creativity can sometimes bemuse others, yet all is dull unless our unique self-expression is free, whether we are understood or not.

Seeker

Fostering was common in Celtic society, especially among wealthier families. Children were sent to relatives of respected people in the community to learn life skills. Bonds between foster children and their guardians were often very strong and thus strengthened relationships between families and within the community. Some children were fostered by leaders within monasteries; the words 'abbot' and 'abbess' derive from the Aramaic *Abba*, the word said to be used by Jesus of God and which means a respected and loved father.

Religious communities were families in Christ and included children, young people and adults who had been brought up within the monastic world. These communities were places where a student might learn to read and write, to chant the psalms and sing, to contribute with manual work, to have self-discipline and respect, and also to love. People could, of course, also seek out a teacher of their own accord, later in life – there are numerous legends of heroes who apprenticed themselves and stories in the lives of the saints about how individuals found themselves drawn to a spiritual life, such as Cuthbert's vision of angelic beings over Lindisfarne, as Aidan lay dying.

Today, we spend many years being guided through a highly structured educational system, but our learning does not end with our school days and our teachers and guides are not all within the school doors. All through life we come across individuals who are wiser and more knowledgeable than we are and from whom we can learn, whether we sit at their feet for a few hours or for many years. Openness of mind to the hunger for truth, for the increase of wisdom, for the deepening of skills, is a lifelong process. Entering into this consciously involves seeking out those who can teach us what we need to know in order to live well, and recognising them when we stumble across them unintentionally. We are never too old!

Householder

In Celtic society, the majority of people lived out their lives according to the customs of the day. Their contact with religion was bound up with rites of passage and the cycles of the agricultural year on which they depended. If there were a monastery or centre of prayer nearby, they might feel more connected with the Christian story than in places where the gospel had not yet made an impact, although, of course, as in all societies, codes of law and justice, loyalties, loves, skills and knowledge were passed on from generation to generation, in a world where survival was much more precarious than it is for most of us in Western society today.

Those touched by the gospel found ways of living their daily lives with a sense of Christ's presence, a hope of God's mercy and a place in heaven. Many of the lives of saints, for example St Brigid and St Patrick, are descriptive of people's early days with their families or foster families – their work in the dairy or the sheep fields, or whatever their situation in life asked of them, sustained through arduous days by prayer, their desire to show love to others unwavering. This was in many ways the group that kept society functioning by their work, skills and productivity, and by their generosity. There was a definite and respected place for those who lived this honest, down-to-earth life, who played their part in maintaining the fabric of a community and keeping the trade routes open, on which everybody depended for travel and the spread of news and culture.

Today, most of us live in a largely secular world. If we are brought up to draw on the gospel for strength, or if we turn to it of our own accord, we each find our own ways of weaving faith in with the demands of daily life and the natural turning of the years. Many strive to live an 'ordinary' life as well as they can, valuing the guidance and care of those who devote all their time to prayer, but finding their own spirituality in the rhythms and activity of daily living in family, in community, at work, in town, on the land. Such characters know the tensions between responsibility for others, the practical implications of showing love in the real world and the need to be free; between hard work earning a living and the blessing of time to think, to reflect and to pray.

Warrior-king or queen

In the Iron Age society in which the Celtic Church grew, local leaders needed to be brave warlords (or warwomen such as Boudicca) as well as wise dispensers of justice in order to hold on to their positions and protect their lands and the lives of the people dependent on the land. Young men commonly became warriors or took up arms when needed, and loyalty to a leader was generously rewarded. Life was often violent and short.

The nominal religion of a whole region could change because of the king. Bede describes the debates of several kings with their elders – for example, Edwin – concerning whether or not they and therefore their people should embrace Christianity. It was often not a matter for personal choice. The pre-Christian codes of conduct for the ruling classes demanded that kings act for the well-being of their subjects, and decisions were not taken lightly.

As kingdoms turned to Christianity, the established ways of ruling, and also the established ways of living daily life, somehow had to be woven in with the teachings of the gospel – a challenge we still face. The Northumbrian Kings Oswald and Oswin, brought up on Iona, were two such warriors who took their Christian faith very seriously, and they engaged Aidan to help them bring Christianity to the region.

Today, although our society is structured differently, there are still powerful leaders whose decisions make an impact on the lives of many. Church leaders make pronouncements and rulings with which their subordinates are expected to comply, despite personal conscience, as do politicians, heads of businesses and so on. Battles, sadly, are sometimes still real wars, into which a whole people get dragged whether they approve or not. What we believe is manipulated, too; the dominant religion today is seen by many as the Economy. Tribalism continues as people fear for their own interests in a turbulent world.

We can experience this wielding of power as ordinary people, subject as we are to the decisions of others who may or may not be acting in our interests, but at times, depending on our situation, we can also be the ones who are making the decisions – even in simple acts such as turning out to vote.

Those holding leadership positions while seeking to follow Christ face a great challenge, not least the judgement of others in the face of Jesus' call to loving service. There are inevitably tensions, conflicts about ideals and values, demands for compromise. All too aware of the harsh real world, one might hold on to the aspiration of something better offered by the gospel message, seeking peace when this is possible but also forgiveness for the violence, the conflict that is sometimes inevitable.

Journaling

When you have chosen a character, write down which one and why you chose it. If you find it difficult to choose, write the words on eight cards and pick one at random. As you work through the book, you might like to refer back to this character and ask yourself whether it affects your perspective, the direction you take, and how it relates to the unfolding story of your life. It might be that as you progress through the book you want to draw in other archetypes which express aspects of yourself. You might also enjoy spotting characters around you who personify these archetypes in different ways.

Having chosen, turn to the prayer for that persona, below, and write that down, too. Change it to suit you better if you like. Journaling examples follow the prayers.

Hermit's prayer

May your presence be sufficient for me,
O Triune God.
May your peace dwell within me,
your wisdom help me,
I in my quiet place,
in the cell of my heart.
Amen

Wandering evangelist's prayer

Watch over me
O Chief of the Elements.
Bear me along in safety
and set me on a fair course,
that I may go where you want me to go
and see what you want me to see,

trusting always in your deep love,
trusting always in your guiding Spirit.
Amen

Abbot/abbess' prayer

So many trust in me,
yet may I trust in you;
so many turn to me,
yet turn I to you,
O Love of all loves,
O Wisdom beyond measure.
Amen

Anamchara's prayer

Jesus Christ come,
and Holy Spirit come,
and Source of All come to be with me
as I am with this child of your grace,
all for love of your love, O companion of tenderness,
all for love of your love.
Amen

Sacred poet's prayer

Be my inspiration,
O Creator of wonders,
O Creator of earth, sea and sky.
May your Spirit breathe through me,
and I not obstruct the way;
may your love shine through me,
and I not cloud your glory.
Amen

Seeker's prayer

O my soul's friend,
guide me to the one who can speak your word.
Open my mind to the one
who can teach what I need to learn,
so I may grow in the strength of your love,
so I may grow and be of use in the world.
Amen

Householder's prayer

O God of my days and nights,
O Christ of my working and resting,
O Spirit of kindness and strength,
my own intention, my own toil,
bless my home, my work and my loved ones,
and give me a generous heart,
a sound head and capable hands to serve you
and to praise you in all that I do.
Amen

Warrior's prayer

Holy one, help me,
blessed one, strengthen me,
beautiful one, forgive me,
glorious one, guide me,
gracious one, hold me
when all is said and done.
Loving one, heal me
when battle is lost or won.
Amen

Journaling examples

Here are a couple of journaling examples which may help your journaling take shape, especially if you haven't settled on a character yet.

I chose the wandering evangelist as my character. I have been thinking about training as a lay chaplain or a street pastor, something voluntary that will get me out talking to people. I did some mission work years ago, but I think I was too young. I used to get into arguments and would feel upset if people didn't want to see things my way. I stopped because I realised I had real anger towards people who didn't want to listen. But this is about something else; it helps me get back to what is important but in a gentler way. I see now that it's more about finding Christ in the other – Christ in friend and stranger.

Or

I was struggling until I got to 'warrior', then I realised, 'Yes that's me. I've been fighting all the way!' It's not completely true – I hate the idea of war and bloodshed as much as anybody – but I know I feel a kind of welling up inside sometimes, especially when I can see someone has been treated wrongly, and I want to get involved – I want to put all my energy into helping them. I don't notice what it costs me until afterwards, but I prefer to have a few scars to that awful feeling of weakness I get if I haven't bothered to try.

I do feel that spiritual people are often a bit unrealistic about the way the world works – they want everything to be peaceful, but it just doesn't work like that. If we don't stand up we really do get walked all over, and then what happens is that the bullies take control. Somebody needs to create safe space. There's no right answer; this is not an ideal world – it's broken and imperfect and sinful and we can only hope to God that we are making choices that have some potential for good in them and that God forgives us when we get it wrong. I really hold on to the vision of a better world where violence is no more, and I really long for God to transform everything, but for now I am not being true to myself if I just sit back and hope God will stop the tyrants of the world while I do and say nothing. I value freedom too much.

Connection with the eight inclinations

There are connections between the archetypes above and the eight inclinations described in chapter 1. We are each unique interweavings of both the archetypes and the inclinations so there are multiple possibilities, but the correspondence chart below summarises the way I see the clearest connections.

Inclination	Picture example	Human archetype
1. Circle, centre, horizontal	Cave by sea in sun or moonlight	Hermit
2. Circle, circumference, horizontal	Village by lake in sun or moonlight	Householder
3. Circle, centre, vertical	Cave on mountainside in sun or moonlight	Sacred poet
4. Circle, circumference, vertical	Village in the mountains in sunshine	Wandering evangelist
5. Cross, centre, horizontal	Cave on seashore with path along the cliff	Seeker
6. Cross, circumference, horizontal	Village on a crossroads by a lake	Warrior king or queen
7. Cross, centre, vertical	Cave beside a mountain stream	*Anamchara*
8. Cross, circumference, vertical	Village on the banks of a river, with trees	Abbot or abbess

Some questions for reflection

- How do your own choices compare with the suggested correspondences above? Are you a justice-campaigning householder, a hermit in the middle of a city?

- If you notice a particular incongruence, how does the tension work out in your own life? It may be that circumstances require you to be more social or more often alone than you would like. You may have a job that affects many of your decisions and actions, or you may be living with constraints that have been imposed on you, such as the requirement to hold a particular belief or to be seen to behave in a particular way. Identifying and working with such tensions may be one of your aims as you work through this book.

- Do negative traits feature strongly in your life experience, such as wandering aimlessly or experiencing rejection by community? If so, it may be helpful to consider talking or working issues through in other ways with a trusted listener as part of your process.

Remember to record your thoughts in your journal before moving on.

Part 2

Where am I?

Chapter 4
Finding our bearings

In the first part, 'Who am I?', we reflected on questions of identity. We now start to consider the spiritual journey itself, and how we locate ourselves in our environment, using the Celtic cross as a guide. There are two ways of looking at the Celtic cross, which can help us get our bearings: vertical and horizontal. We will explore both.

Initially, we are going to consider natural features of landscape, because the earth beneath us is always our home, whatever is built up around us. We will then go on to think about how this translates to a more urban setting. Reflecting on the landscape which underlies the towns and cities in which most of us live enables us to see our location with new eyes. A hill is still a hill, whether it has an estate built on it or not. A river may be redirected underneath or round the back of a shopping centre, but it is still flowing. A road may be made of asphalt now, and wide enough for four lanes of traffic, but it is still a pathway: indeed, it may be an ancient drover's road, a strategic Roman road, a prehistoric hunting trail. Likewise, the people we pass are not coracle makers, wandering monks and hymn-writing farm hands, on the whole, but they each are on their own life journey, like their ancestors before them.

The upright cross

Steadfast love and faithfulness will meet;
righteousness and peace will kiss each other.
Faithfulness will spring up from the ground,
and righteousness will look down from the sky.

Psalm 85:10-11

We start with an upright view of the cross in a prominent place – up on a hill, at a grave, at a crossroads or a boundary, on the site of an old church. This is a cross that acts as a landmark, like a standing stone inserted into the landscape by particular people long gone and for a particular reason, now obscure. This view of the cross is like a pin stuck in a map – 'I know exactly where I am; I am at the old Celtic cross!'

Pause for a moment and imagine such a Celtic cross, perhaps one you have seen yourself. How tall is it? How is it decorated? Why do you imagine it was put in that place? What is its location?

Now imagine that you are there with that cross. (If you prefer, think about a cross you have visited or one you have seen a photo of, and ask yourself what attracts you to visit it.) Why are you there? Are you an inquisitive sightseer? A pilgrim? A traveller passing by? A visitor come to pay your respects in a graveyard? Are you actually there reluctantly?

Your reasons for being there can tell you something about yourself and your spiritual journey. Perhaps you are just exploring, looking around, wanting to find out about history and culture; perhaps you feel drawn to the sense of community with the past, or maybe you are on the way somewhere, even mysteriously led or pushed to the place where you find yourself. You may even be back in childhood, brought out on a family excursion, and you are at the cross because it means something to somebody else, especially your parents.

Take time to reflect on the imaginary scene of this Celtic cross, or a memory or image that is special to you, and make notes on your thoughts before you move on. Remember also to consider connections in location with the inclinations in chapter 1.

Journaling examples

Here are two contrasting examples, if it helps to have a model for writing your own notes:

> I remember the old Celtic cross in the graveyard at Nevern in Wales. It is tall and beautifully carved with panels of knotwork. I trace my fingers over the stone, wondering what hands chiselled the pattern so skilfully, so long ago. I have visited this place several times before. The first time, in my childhood, we went because my parents were interested in ancient history. I am drawn back by the cross and the old yew trees, and the Ogham inscriptions inside the church.
>
> Today, although we are on the way somewhere, we have made a special detour to come here and be quiet for a while. It's a little pilgrimage. I sense something special about the place; I am drawn to the intertwining of ancient trees and ancient human presence, the dark, quiet mystery of the place. I sit, as though listening. I want the stone and the trees and the little birds to tell me something I feel as though I have forgotten, about Christ, about humanity, about creation.

I notice that I am willing to go out of my way, drawn by something I can't quite explain, with a sense of deep listening, listening as though for a distant voice or an echo, something just too low or too high for me normally to hear . . . and I notice that I owe something to my parents for giving me a fascination with the ancient.

Or

I imagine a Celtic cross which I can see up on the ridge of a hill, silhouetted against the skyline. To get there, I need to walk up a narrow track through the heather, which many have walked before. I follow in their footsteps with reverence.

I am glad to have reached the cross. I have been walking a long time and evening is approaching. I know that from the cross I will be able to see down into the next valley, where I can find rest and shelter for the night. I am tired and the cross seems to welcome me as a companion. I sit with my back against it, eating an apple. It is as though the cross has always been here, a protective outstretching of wide arms, a message of love extending in all directions.

I notice that I am on the way somewhere, that I feel quite tired but at peace, that I find comfort, welcome and protection in the presence of the cross. It helps me to extend love outwards, too, in the direction I am heading, and in the direction I have come from.

The cross as a map

Thus says the Lord:
Stand at the crossroads, and look,
and ask for the ancient paths,
where the good way lies; and walk in it,
and find rest for your souls.
But they said, 'We will not walk in it.'

Jeremiah 6:16

Draw a large Celtic cross on a sheet of paper and lay it flat, like a map of a crossroads with an orbital road, the paths continuing beyond the circle in the four directions, one going further than the others. Consider making a really big cross on the ground that you (and others) can walk around, perhaps using long ropes, or traced out on a sandy beach. Think, too, about orientation: consider using a compass to align your cross with the Poles.

Having drawn your cross, take time to trace the lines with a finger, randomly, to see where they lead, what directions you find yourself going in. If you have the space and time to make a large one, walk the map meditatively, like a labyrinth but with more freedom to choose your route as you come to each crossroads. As you walk, or finger-walk, try chanting an adaptation of the Jeremiah quote above:

Stand at the crossroads and look, and ask for the ancient paths.
Ask where the good way lies and walk that way,
and so find rest for your soul.

As you contemplate the pathways of the cross, you might start to get a feeling about how they reflect your own situation, the pathways of your spiritual journey. Where do you find yourself pausing? Where do you begin to feel impatient? Perhaps you decide to go off road into one of the spaces or notice that your path is sloping uphill or down. Perhaps you see yourself at the centre asking, 'Which way now?' or out on the edge, wondering, 'Am I just going round in circles?' You might be heading inwards or coming from a particular direction, north, south, east or west. Those directions can have special significance for us, which we will explore below.

Some descriptions follow, to help you locate yourself on the cross map. Each description also has a prayer. Read them and notice which ones resonate with you. For this set of descriptions I draw on Christian as well as natural observations for the symbolic value of the directions, which are of significance to many who walk an earth–spirituality path. (Correspondences with times and seasons will come later in the book.)

When you have read the descriptions, make a note of the one you feel describes your situation best, and add this prayer to the prayers you chose for your identity.

Location descriptors

The paths

The paths of the Celtic cross map were made by our spiritual ancestors who walked that way ahead of us. Following in their footsteps, we tread holy ground and discover many of the things that they experienced, in new ways. We can sense their companionship still, so that our inner solitude is not lonely but rich in love. At times, though, a path can become a drudgery, plodding on and on; we can walk reluctantly, even feel that we are being compelled against our will. We can rush and not notice our environment, miss signs, become distracted from the present moment by worrying about reaching our destination or the place we have left behind. Notice your mood as you contemplate the map and your journeying, and take time to write about it.

God be with me in every path,
Christ be with me each step I take,
Spirit speed me, Spirit guide me,
the Holy Three for company,
the Holy One never leaving me.
Amen

East

In the Christian faith, the east is of great significance. The rising sun is the symbol par excellence of the 'rising Son', the mystery of the resurrection. For centuries, churches have been built with the altar and the congregation facing east. Traditionally, the priest faced (or faces) east too, elevating the bread and wine in the direction of the dawn on behalf of the people. It is a direction of hope and renewal. Facing east, we are aligned with the faithful through the ages, the communion of the saints (which we explore in a later chapter), to a sacred path full of joy. If you are *in* the east, you are in a place of renewal and expectation.

Light of all lights,
Christ of newness and of morning joy,
breathe your gladness into me
and let my way be blessed.
Amen

South

This is the direction of the midday sun, a time of maximum power. The sun's energy is the source of all our energy on earth; it is the reason why we have life, but it also has the power to destroy life. It is a worldwide symbol of God who is 'a sun and shield' (Psalm 84:11). Facing south or walking a path heading south, you have the sun right ahead of you, shining in your eyes and casting a shadow behind you. This might make the journey uncomfortable, with too much heat and light. Yet plants grow up towards the sun, and perhaps that is how you see yourself right now. If you are *in* the south, you are in a place of high energy, maximum power and productivity, which may be quite hard work but also high yield.

O God of all creation,
may I never cease to wonder at your works
nor doubt the glory of your radiance;
so keep me strong and full of courage,
you my guide and you my shield,
and you the eternal sun of my sky,
you the bright and lovely sun of my sky.
Amen

West

This is the direction where the sun goes down. The term 'to go west' is a euphemism for dying, although when we come to the chapter on spiritual companions, we will find St Brendan making an amazing voyage westward from Ireland to a paradise-like place and living to tell the tale. So it can be a direction of dreams and visions, of inner journeying as well as outer exploration, a hunger to learn more about creation and be touched by wonder. West is a direction of maturity and gentle decline in energy. It can be one of the most beautiful directions to look in, as the sun begins to set. Heading west, you are heading to a place of maturation where you can pause to mull over the experiences in your life and gain wisdom, or take a well-earned rest to find a new perspective. If you are *in* the west, you might be enjoying a time of reflection, of reaping the benefits of past efforts. You may also be noticing a natural ebbing of energy.

Peace, I seek,
O gentle Shepherd of the way;
wisdom and patience I would learn
from the journey and the many that I meet
on the long paradise road
of my walk with you.
Amen

North

This is the direction in the sky where we do not see the sun. In the northern hemisphere, the north wind is a cold wind which drives us indoors or sends us to put on warmer clothes. North is associated with the inhospitable, with endurance. It can be a place of hardship and testing, but it can also be a place of retreat, patiently biding time until conditions improve and the journey can begin again. If you are facing north (when the sun is out) you are fully aware of your shadow, which may loom large in front of you. You may be heading down an arduous path, which will stretch you to your limits, but this is not necessarily something you can or should avoid. If you are *in* the north, you may feel that you are experiencing something of an ordeal, even wrestling with issues of finality or mortality, yet in that struggle you may also be surprised by elements of great beauty.

Christ, shield me,
God of goodness, shield me,
Spirit holy, shield me
while I make my way,
and draw me to the refuge
of your warmth,
the refuge of the Holy Three,
the refuge of the Holy One of love.
Amen

Centre of circle

This can be a beautiful and still place, the eye of the storm or the still centre, the axle of a wheel turning round and round. It can be a place of interior peace, of 'centredness' where we experience the present moment free of all the complications of everyday life. It can be the interior room of prayer where we go for intimacy with God, or the love we feel when we are connected to another very deeply. It can be the summit of a mountain where it feels that we are on top of the world, a view all around, or the centre of a labyrinth, a moment of arrival, of pause, before retracing our steps. If you are heading towards the centre you might be drawn by or seeking a deep love which may have a mystical quality to it, or by a feeling that for the moment at least, everything makes sense. If you are *in* the centre, you may be experiencing great peace and joy, a sense of union with the Divine and with creation.

O Love of all loves,
a shade you are in the heat,
a hearth fire you are in the cold,
a spring you are in dry land
a bower you are for the beloved.
So I come to you in joy,
and you to me, O Love,
and you to me.
Amen

Crossroads

Although the centre of the circle and the crossroads may be the same point, there are also four crossroads in the Celtic cross map where the straight paths intersect with the circular path. Crossroads are rich in symbolism, places where we exercise our freedom of choice, but they are also places where we often suffer with indecision, uncertainty or lack of clarity. What if we make the wrong decision? People of faith sometimes worry that they cannot tell which way God wants them to go. Such anxieties come to a head here. But the deep peace of the circle centre is at the heart of this place, whether we can feel it or not. The agony of exercising our freedom to choose is held in love. We are free; there is no single 'right' path, nor a single 'wrong' path: the map offers many possibilities, including straying off the path. If you are approaching a crossroads you may be wondering, 'Which way now?' Likewise, if you are at a crossroads but you pause and connect for a moment with the circle centre of deep love, you might feel your decisions are made a little more easily.

God be with me, protecting my way,
Spirit be with me, guiding my way,
and Christ be with me wherever I go,
redeeming my choices
and reminding me of love,
though I may stray or fall,
though I may stray or fall many a time
before I find the way, but never alone.
Amen

The orbital path

This path can be seen to describe the journey of the sun in the
sky – but also the earth's journey around the sun, or our
journey through life. It seems to be a circle, but time being
what it is, nothing is ever quite the same the second time
around. Revisiting, we see new details, changes, developments,
so a spiral might be a better way of seeing the path. Cycles can
seem predictable; we may feel we are trapped, caught in a rut,
even destined for something inevitable, or we may feel safe
because we can see what is coming next – we understand the
pattern or the routine. Nothing is pre-ordained for us: we can
exit the cycle and go wherever we choose, although some
directions are easier or wiser than others.

I walk this path
as I have walked this path before,
and ancient is the way,
and ancient steps guide mine,
and ancient are you, O Love,
yet just newborn.
Ancient are you, O Life
yet just newborn.
Amen

In between and beyond

The spaces between and beyond the roads are the environment itself. If you feel that your location at the moment is off road, then trust that intuition and, as with places on the path, write down your thoughts about how that place feels. It might be that for now, you are exploring the spirituality of the natural world with a sense of freedom, wishing to let the environment teach you directly. It might be that you feel frustration with the paths that you know, or feel lost or confused. All these feelings are part of the spiritual journey, and recognising them is an important part of understanding ourselves.

Wherever I am, you know it, O God.
Though I may fall, I am held;
though lost, I am found.
Wherever I am, O God, you see me from within,
and I am safe in you,
and you are safe in my heart.
Amen

Journaling

When you have spent time with your Celtic cross map and the direction descriptions, go back to the description that best matches where you are at the moment, make notes on why you chose this and add the prayer for that direction to your notes.

Take time also to consider how your reflections in this chapter relate to your response at the beginning, to the personal perspectives on the Celtic cross in chapter 1.

These inclinations are represented with pictures of locations in which the presence or absence of paths and crossroads have significance. If you felt a strong interest in one of the four directions you might be able to give an orientation to your inclination picture – where does the sun rise and set?

Here are examples of reflections on direction for inspiration:

I chose north in the end, but north facing east. I feel as though I've been through a really difficult time lately – all I've wanted to do is hide away, but some things just can't be left so I've struggled to keep going. I was starting to feel quite low, drained, and well . . . just fed up and in need of a rest. But I thought the other day about that verse in Hosea – I must look it up – how dawn always comes in the end, and that cheered me up. That's why I say I'm facing east – I'm waiting for the dawn and it gives me hope every day that things are going to get easier soon. So for now, this is my prayer:

Christ, shield me,
God of goodness, shield me,
Spirit holy, shield me
while I make my way,
and draw me to the refuge
of your warmth,
the refuge of the Holy Three,
the refuge of the Holy One of love.
Amen

Or

I chose 'in between and beyond'. I have really moved away from mainstream faith over the last few years. I stopped knowing who to trust or who to listen to and decided I needed to get away from all these voices to work out what I really think. I find a great deal of peace and healing in nature – cycling or walking or even watching nature documentaries. I'm sure it's saying something to me, as though there's a truth I need to uncover. I feel I haven't worked out what it is yet, but I'm constantly drawn outdoors, almost as though creation's calling me. I'm a bit worried about losing touch completely with my faith, but somehow I feel Christ's with me 'off road' without any need for words. So the prayer I'm using for now is this, but I have changed 'God' to 'Christ' – somehow I feel more connected to the word 'Christ':

Wherever I am, you know it, O Christ.
Though I may fall, I am held,
though lost, I am found.
Wherever I am, O Christ, you see me from within,
and I am safe in you,
and you are safe in my heart.
Amen

Meditation on the streets

'I will rise now and go about the city,
in the streets and in the squares;
I will seek him whom my soul loves.'
I sought him, but found him not.
The sentinels found me,
as they went about in the city.
'Have you seen him whom my soul loves?'
Scarcely had I passed them,
when I found him whom my soul loves.
I held him, and would not let him go
until I brought him into my mother's house,
and into the chamber of her that conceived me.

Song of Songs 3:2-4

Before you go any further, find time to root your reflections in the real world (with due care and attention to road safety!). Engaging mindfully means with a relaxed but also a *heightened* awareness of your environment.

The Celtic cross can be found all over the place in built-up areas, wherever there is a roundabout at a crossroads. Look out for a place where it is safe (dropped kerbs? traffic lights?) and comfortable to walk or use a mobility vehicle. A dual carriageway roundabout on the ring road is obviously not the best place, but there may well be a mini roundabout somewhere near, or a pedestrianised shopping centre with side streets, where you can make out a rough circle and roads leading in four directions. Use maps to help you.

As a creative alternative, you could work out a public transport route defining a circle and cross, and make a day – or several days – of it, travelling around the city. The London

Underground is full of exciting potential, and many big towns and cities have an orbital bus route plus ways of travelling on a north–south line and an east–west line. Plan how to link the routes up, and at which points you need to go back on yourself.

This is an activity to engage with as fully as you can in the present moment, and to lay aside all the things you usually fill your mind with as you travel. Consider taking a notebook or a voice recorder, to help your journal entry later.

When you have found a suitable place, decide how to travel to it. If possible, avoid using a car as this has to occupy your full attention, whereas taking public transport will allow you freedom to look around and notice the people and little details. From the minute you set out, you are making an intentional journey, a little pilgrimage. Be aware of what is going on, creatures you see, people you pass, road signs, buildings, bridges, signs of decay and newness . . .

When you reach the site you have chosen, pause to get your bearings and to make sure the place is as safe for walking as you had anticipated. Where is the sun? Which way is north? What do the road signs say? What lies in each direction, within view and further away?

Start walking mindfully, noticing everything, even if it is a very familiar place. Notice flowers in gardens and weeds in cracks; notice birdsong; notice parents with children; notice road workers; notice fallen twigs, puddles, water rushing under drain covers, patterns in brickwork, signs you never noticed before; notice where the shadows fall, which way the wind blows, whether you are walking uphill or down; notice your mood. Walk whichever way you like, round the circle first or west, or following the north–south road as far as you like. At what point do you choose to turn and go back?

What, if anything, invites you temporarily off the path? A grassy patch? A tea shop? Go in if you want, but allow the whole encounter to feed your experience of the place rather than distract you from it.

The first time you walk your Celtic cross, do so simply to experience the present moment and to be as aware as you can be of the environment and how it speaks to you, then write about your experience. You might wish to revisit this place another time, perhaps with a companion, to walk it with a focus such as picking up litter, showing kindness to strangers or praying for peace in the neighbourhood, or using a repetitive Celtic prayer – perhaps of protection. Each time you revisit, add to your journal.

Journaling examples

Here are two journal entries to prompt your own. They are a little longer than some of the other journal examples, to give a full picture, and are from real locations.

> Walking north between terraced houses and parked cars, past the old chapel, two beautiful beech trees flank the entrance, the leaves not out yet. Water is leaking from a road cover, in a muddy trickle along the gutter. I reach the centre of the cross, a grassy roundabout. There was an accident here the other day – a car lost control and went right over the roundabout and smashed a hole in the wall on the other side. Passing the corner shop, I peer in to see who's at the till; nobody to say 'Hi' to today. Then I turn right downhill, past the bus stop, past disabled access to a home, with the

constant noise of cars, no front gardens, litter blowing about, large terraced houses – two joined into one, a shared household . . . a road sign says no access to cars on to the main road. I cross over and go back up on the sunny side of the street alongside a cycle lane. Railings protect children at the school. Scraggy trees push through fencing, I'm walking uphill now, bearing west. There's a passer-by in hijab on her phone, a policewoman walks by also on her phone . . .

I'm back at the centre, turning right again . . . passing by the car mechanic. Again I peer in to see if there's anyone to say 'Hello' to, then there's the playground and the teachers' car park. I never like the look of it: triple-parking – who wants to get stuck in there?! My postman friend waves from the other side of the road and asks if I found the parcel he left with a neighbour. I cross at the junction with the main road and walk back up the road, walking towards the sun, past the church centre, a buggy parked outside, then right again going west and more steeply uphill, past the mosque. It's quiet now but it will get busy later, with Friday afternoon prayers. Now I'm crossing over opposite the high school, and I'm going back downhill towards the centre, then I'm going to go home.

Reflection on the recording

As I began transcribing my recording, I wasn't sure how worthwhile the exercise had been. I didn't feel very spiritual and it took me 20 minutes, which was longer than I planned. But look how many people I know in the area well enough for a friendly wave or to stop for a chat – the shopkeepers, who are all lovely;

the postman, also lovely; the mechanics, who are extremely helpful; a lot of the people in the church centre, had I gone inside, and I know the wife of the Imam at the mosque. The locals are part of the walk, and they brighten my day when I see them. Although there is a lot of rubbish on the streets and constant noise of traffic, I passed three huge beech trees, two oaks, a magnolia just starting to come out in deep pink buds, and quite a lot of forsythia in bloom; the sun was out and the sky was blue . . . And what a spiritual area! In about a square half mile, I walked past two Christian places of worship and a Mosque, all thriving. And what a child-friendly area, with a primary school, a high school, the Madrassa at the Mosque and the nursery at the church centre. I feel challenged to reflect more deeply on the goodness in this place, beyond and behind the red brick and tarmac.

Or

I chose this location because it's a nice walk to get there, although I did put my personal alarm in my pocket – it makes me feel a bit safer now I haven't got the dog. Taking the alleyway between the houses at the end of my street, then right on to the riverside path, I am struck by springtime! Birdsong, flowing water, hawthorn starting to green and blackthorn already in blossom . . . how lovely! After a while, the ford and footbridge bring me to the westerly arm of my cross; I liked the idea of a river in the west. I stand on the bridge to collect my thoughts, noticing as I do a couple of number plates lying half submerged in the water following the recent floods. My intention is simply to be open to whatever there is, to see and hear anew. Walking slightly uphill towards the east, I realise I misremembered. The roundabout is at the next junction along! Never mind, this is still a crossroads and there is no traffic about so I walk my own wide circle, clockwise, noticing a little crab apple tree marking the west, a double line of lime trees on the north–south road and an old oak to the east. These semi-detached houses are from the 1930s and I suspect the oak is older – it has 'seen' changes from farmland to suburb in its time.

I am drawn to the sunshine today: it is a real delight after such a dull, rainy winter, so I walk south along the line of limes, noticing the back gardens between the gaps of the houses. There is more greenery around here than meets the eye, and I can hear robins, blackbirds and sparrows, even though I cannot see them. It makes me glad just to know they are there. I walk almost as far as the next junction, quite reluctant to turn away from the sun.

Heading back, north, my shadow is short and well defined before me. If I were to carry on, I would reach the edge of the city centre. From the crossroads, the view west attracts me more, over the river to a playing field and lots of trees – respite from the density of buildings around here.

I have been moved by how much the natural world continues to thrive here. Heading back, I decide to have a look at my 1903 map of the area, to find out more about the land and how it used to be used, to try to get more in touch with the life of the place.

Chapter 5
Inner landscapes and thinness

Then Jacob woke from his sleep and said, 'Surely the Lord is in this place – and I did not know it!' And he was afraid, and said, 'How awesome is this place! This is none other than the house of God, and this is the gate of heaven.'

Genesis 28:16-17

The quotation above is from the account of Jacob's dream of angels ascending and descending a heavenly ladder. The dream makes him realise that he is in a special place and he sets up a stone altar there, calling the place *Beth-el* or 'house of God'. In the Celtic tradition we might call such a place 'thin'. 'Thinness' is a familiar term in Celtic Christianity, and evokes a place that seems to have a quality about it where we feel especially close to God, to the spiritual dimension, to mystery, to our own inner 'knowing': the veil between this world and the spiritual realms is thin.

Different people have different experiences of thinness and also different ideas about what it means. For some, thin places are quite rare and have become holy through centuries of prayer by the faithful. Examples include the islands of Iona and Lindisfarne. To these hallowed places we might add other locations, particularly ancient places of worship or the sites of significant events, many of which are or have been places of pilgrimage, such as old holy wells and chapels. We might add other sites of even older human activity – standing stones, for example.

Others feel that the sanctity of a place is less dependent on a history of human prayer or activity and more on the natural world itself, and on personal experience of the Divine breaking though in moments of awe. Mountains, the seashore and other places where earth and sky or earth and water meet are often described this way, and this is partly why mountains represent the vertical axis and the sea or lake the horizontal in the eight inclinations in chapter 1.

Those of us living in an urban setting, for whom it is not easy to get out to places of natural beauty and spiritual antiquity, seek thin places in the cities, in the streets and in the squares – the art galleries, parks and places of worship.

The possibility of finding thinness increases by taking time to be still and fully present in a place, and to be *quiet* – quiet inside as well as physically quiet. It is perhaps this element which is more challenging to overcome in the city, yet still, we can be surprised by moments and places, as thinness has a lot to do with state of mind. We can feel as much reverence at the sight of a cherry tree covered in blossom in the local park as at the sight of a remote, misty mountain.

Thinness and the city

Most of us cannot be in these soul-nourishing places as often as we would like, but we can hold the beauty in our inner being – whether this is our head, our heart, our belly or our very bones. We can plan special journeys at the same time as exploring the idea of thinness in our immediate settings. We can see the reality of our location – the roads and railways, tower blocks, ports and shopping arcades, the lives lived out in these places – and we can see the underlying reality of place, too – land meets water, buildings towering cliff-like into the sky, flat flood plains spread out on the banks of the river.

With this in mind, it is worth considering why urban settlements grow up where they do. Often it is because a long time ago a special feature was identified, and people gathered to settle. These might include:

- a river ford

- a spring

- a good site for boats to moor

- a crossroads

- an ancient sacred site for rituals, fairs, burials and feasts

- a monastery, where work, food and health care were available

- a sheltered place near a natural resource such as copper or coal

- a site in or on the edge of a wood full of useful timber and food

- a good stopping point on a trade route

- a good trading place

- a hunting party encampment

- a strategic location for a defensive structure

- a place with land and a climate suitable for farming or a particular industry.

Whatever towns and cities may look like today, they are places where people have gradually converged for all sorts of reasons, often in response to features of the land itself. Something of that original quality remains in a place.

Beneath the noise, buildings and bustle, the river is still there. The micro-climate is still there. The strategic lookout point is still there. The spirit of community that drew people together in the first place is still there. A mountain or a river will still be there, although a forest may have gone, its memory and the memory of its creatures in the soil beneath the tarmac.

Finding out something of the history of a settlement can help us appreciate the quality of that place and the continuity of life there – the human struggle, social justice issues, health concerns, the impact of war and plague, immigration and emigration patterns, trade, industry, economic depression, shared struggle, victories in matters of equality and welfare . . . Loving humanity does not stop with our immediate neighbours; it stretches into the past and the future and all around the world. Into our cities, people come from all around the world. Our outreach in love, or our struggle to love, is the new chapter in the history of our settlements.

Although cities may lack the feeling of expansiveness and freedom of open countryside or seascape, because of the facilities, it can be quite easy to live a relatively environmentally friendly lifestyle. In the British Isles at least, there are few places that have not been shaped by human intervention. The rolling hills and pastures that some of us can sometimes be guilty of romanticising are other people's places of hard work – or lack of it. They used to have trees on them. The now somnolent canals were dug out at huge cost to life a few hundred years ago. In ancient times, the land used to be very difficult to travel, so much of it was marsh or wildwood. It was considered safer to travel by boat along the rivers and around the coast than by land, a fact reflected in the abundance of accounts of Celtic coracle and curragh journeys. Habitations have come and gone; plagues have wiped out populations; land clearance acts, tyrants and greedy landlords have destroyed whole communities; battles have been fought; monocultures have eliminated hedgerows and endangered species . . .

If we stop to find out about and reflect on the social history of an area of countryside, we can find ourselves as emotionally challenged as if we were looking out over a noisy, grubby city. For the same reasons, we can be as uplifted by looking out over a city, or encountering some aspect of the city, as we can by spending time in beautiful countryside. We can walk through a natural habitat unmoved and unaware, and we can walk through a town fully alive to the presence of the Divine. It depends on what is going on in our hearts, guts and heads, and deep in our bones.

One of the ways we can connect, if at a loss, in a very urban area is by looking for tiny signs of life. An ant in a paving stone crack can bring joy. Another way is to look up, to look at the sky and the birds. It seems that some species of birds see the buildings differently to us. They see them as big cliffs. So we get pigeons – feral rock doves – and we get seagulls, starlings and sparrows, even raptors, preying on the rest. We have built desert-like habitats, strange ones, and over time, animals and plants work out ways of adapting to them.

Journaling and examples

Pause now, and think about your own experiences of 'thinness'. If you wish, as always, link this back to your choice of picture location in chapter 1. Here are some journal examples:

I live in the city. I work in the city. Once a year I pay quite a lot of money to travel up to Scotland to go on retreat, and this is always something I look forward to. I start to hunger for the wide open space – I think that's what really gets to me. The minute I get into the mountainous areas, my soul lifts. I feel a huge weight lift off my shoulders like a bird taking off in flight. That's something to do with thinness – the sense of that big heavy bird on my shoulders flapping its wings and soaring up into the sky.

I usually go to Iona, which I do love, but now I come to think of it, the feeling of spiritual freedom hits me before I get anywhere near Iona. I arrive already far more at peace than when I set out. Being there is a kind of consolation. I pray and take part in worship, sometimes do organised retreats, and I feel something almost indescribable about the connection to people stretching back over the last century, rebuilding this place, and then way back in time to the centre it used to be. How amazing, to put my feet where Columba himself stood! What an immense link to sanctity!

Then when I have to come back the bird gradually comes back to my shoulder and the weight returns. It always happens, I rarely want to leave. Knowing I can come back keeps me going through the year.

Thinking about thinness in the city is difficult. I have been resisting the idea. I don't really like the city; I'm here because I have to be not because I want to be, and 'escape plans' feature quite highly. I guess I feel hemmed in, and as an introvert I struggle with the noise and bustle and all the people. Then, the other day, we had a work meeting in a different room to usual, up on the ninth floor, and as soon as I walked into the room I was bowled over by the view out of the window – a huge window, the length of the room. I could see right over the city: the rooftops were like rocky outcrops, and seagulls were swooping and soaring in the setting sun. It was spectacular. Just for a while, I felt that sense of freedom. I was out there with the seagulls, seeing the city from a completely different perspective. Amazing! Maybe that window is a window to thinness for me.

Or

I love ancient places. I am interested in history and like to imagine how things used to be, the people who lived in a place long ago. There are particular buildings that really get to me and I try to visit if I'm passing. One is the crypt at Worcester Cathedral; another, a tiny medieval church in a village near a wood up the road from the garden centre. I like to go in and sit in a pew and imagine the people through the ages. I love the fact that they leave the church open for visitors. Sometimes I sit in the cemetery and think about all the lives, all the loves.

Then there are pathways, too. I find walking the Ridgeway near the White Horse at Uffington incredibly powerful – it's the idea of my footsteps on the same path as people over thousands of years. And there's a flagstone trackway over the hills that I've walked several times, laid by quarry workers maybe two centuries ago, trudging to work and back, day in, day out.

It's the connection to humanity that seems to affect me. In town, I go down to the canal and think about the navvies who dug it out, the fuss people made about progress, how little idea they had about what was to come in the future. I look at building sites and wonder how much things are going to change in our future. As for thinness, I think it's wherever my imagination starts to work, showing me pictures of people's lives, what mattered to them, how hard life was, what brought them joy and pain, what gave them hope. I have a sense of love for humanity in those moments, of understanding, of knowing how important it is to have compassion. It makes me think of Jesus looking over the city, weeping and saying he wishes to gather everybody up and give them peace.

Pause in the journey

It is now time to pause again and consider the journey so far, and what lies ahead. Using a Celtic Christian outlook and the idea of the Celtic cross as a life map, you have reflected on your identity – Who am I? – and your location and the wider environment in which you find yourself – Where am I? You have had the opportunity to collect prayers and biblical passages that reflect your personal response to how you see yourself at the moment.

This is a good time to read over your journal and update it with thoughts, pictures or anything else that has spoken to you along the way. In particular, reflect on your initial response in chapter 1, and how the inclination you settled on relates to your thoughts on a place. Remember, each inclination has a picture of a location, made up of symbolic elements:

- a tree or mountain

- a path or river

- a solitary hut or cave or a settlement

- the presence of sun or moon – indicators of direction.

You might enjoy imagining yourself into or drawing your personal location picture and exploring where the paths and rivers lead, what the view from the mountain looks like, what the cave is like inside, what direction the vista faces, where the shadows fall, what creatures share this place, what the climate is like, and so on.

Staying put in one place

Am I a God near by, says the Lord, and not a God far off?
Who can hide in secret places so that I cannot see them? says the
Lord. Do I not fill heaven and earth? says the Lord.

Jeremiah 23:23-24

We have thought a lot about journeying along the pathways and spaces of the Celtic cross as we live out the stories of our lives, but there is also a time to stay put.

Although many Celtic saints travelled a good deal and are famous for their voyages, the vocation of a brother or sister in a monastery invariably began with years of rigorous training in the contemplative life. The rule of life in such places revolved around the continuous cycle of daily prayer, and chanting or reciting the psalms and liturgies in harmony with the passing hours and turning seasons. The monastery was a hub, a centre point around which a community revolved, and many never left the shelter of these places. The pattern for this existence was that of the Desert Fathers and Mothers themselves, who lived as hermits or in small praying communities in remote, wild places around the Mediterranean.

One of the most well-known and respected monks of the era, on whom we rely for a good deal of information on the Celtic saints, was an Anglo Saxon rather than a Celt – the Venerable Bede. He wrote many erudite volumes of history, natural history and other texts, worked out the pattern of the tides and their relationship to the moon, and calculated the dates of the equinoxes. He hardly moved, all his long life, from his monastery at Jarrow in Northumbria.

This spirit of staying put is expressed by a respected abbess, Samthann of Clonbroney in Ireland, who is described more fully later on. She told someone preparing for pilgrimage that there was no need to go anywhere to experience the presence of God, since God is close wherever we are.

Even a saint such as Brendan, who pre-dates Samthann and who is also described more fully later on, famous for his voyage west, apparently over the Atlantic Ocean, spent most of his life quietly and prayerfully in religious community with his brothers, before setting off in his later years on the adventure of a lifetime. His journey makes fascinating reading, and it was defined (as we will see) by the patterns of the liturgical year, and by prayer. His unshakeable confidence in Christ was anchored in his deep prayer life; the calm centredness of the true contemplative was always in St Brendan's heart.

In St Brendan's travels, a great part of his motivation was to discover new marvels in the natural world, which enhanced his sense of wonder in the Creator. But while he was seeking new wonders beyond him, paradise even, there was a strong sense of God's presence with him all the while, protecting him, guiding him, providing for his needs. Experience of God is not simply an aspiration for something in the future; it is also an ever-present reality, whether in a little boat or a monastic cell.

It tends to be a characteristic of the Celtic worldview to find the Divine immersed in or revealed by creation, as in the joyous discoveries of St Brendan as he encountered icebergs, whales and islands of beautiful birds. There are, of course, different theological positions on the presence of God in creation, just as there are different attitudes to the practice of contemplative prayer and devotion to a rule of life. When we find ourselves focusing on the immediacy of our location, our response to the environment around us and our notion of God's presence depends a lot on our wider outlook on life. Not everybody is a natural contemplative, as we considered in chapter 1.

Journaling

Before we explore further, pause to write about your thoughts on this section so far. Consider especially your approach to prayer and your feelings about the presence of God in the world.

Here are some questions which you may like to consider:

- Where, if at all, is God in the world?

- Does God's presence in creation make it holy, or is it human prayer and worship that draws down the holy?

- What is the value of prayer, and what styles of prayer do you feel most drawn to?

- When you settled on one of eight inclinations in chapter 1, were you more drawn to the solitary or community, to inner reflection or outer engagement with others? Does your initial choice still reflect your current thoughts and feelings?

- What could you create on the theme of God's indwelling presence, centredness, sanctity, creation, or one of the other themes in this section that has stood out strongly for you?

Here are some prayers, if you would like to add them to your collection:

God of grace,
forgive my ignorance and grant me wisdom.
Christ of love,
open my mind, and open my heart.
Spirit of truth,
guide me and fill me with your clarity,
that I may understand what you want me to understand,
see what you want me to see,
know what you want me to know,
all for love,
all for goodness,
all for your perfect and beautiful will,
O most Holy One.
Amen

O Creator God,
nothing gives me so much peace
as to sit a while in a green place
or down by the seashore
and to watch and listen,
and in that place, in that peace,
I find you anew,
and with delight I carry you back
to the everyday.
There, too, you give me peace,
and in my peace, others find peace.
Amen

Change and challenge

Pausing long enough to become familiar with a location, we find that this place, too, is never static. There is newness and decay all around us, and the changing times, weather and seasons in turn bring their own changes, just as people and animals come and go. The world seems to revolve all around us. We will think more later on about the journey through times and seasons and the people who become our companions along the way.

In the Celtic tradition, both journey and settling in one place, or visiting for a significant period, were important. Some made travelling their vocation; others travelled to a particular place and then stopped to build a place of prayer – an oratory – to join an existing community or to make a simple dwelling for themselves. Once it was known that a holy person had arrived in an area, people would come seeking their wisdom and their prayers, and centres would grow up around them. Each would become, perhaps, the centre of a circle, defined by the cross. Those more inclined towards a solitary lifestyle, such as St Kevin on Glendalough, would then take off again, further into the wilderness, although they would keep an occasional eye on the community that had gathered because of them – as, in turn, the community kept a prayerful eye on them. This pattern follows that of the Desert Fathers and Mothers of the Northern African region up through the Holy Land to Syria. These people left the cities in response to the empire building of Constantine, seeking not the grandeur and status that was absorbing institutional Christianity, but austerity and soul searching.

Austerity and soul searching are not always attractive elements of spiritual practice. In today's world, where we can design our own spiritual paths to suit our own inclinations, there is a strong temptation to avoid anything that sounds so arduous. Yet it is in these 'desert' or wilderness places that real transformation often happens, and some of the places where we end up do reflect something of the desert. For the Celtic saints, as we shall consider below, deserts were wildwood, cliff cave or remote island; the centre of their world was their simple stone or wooden cell.

Jesus, although he spent time in the wilderness, came into the towns and villages to meet people in their everyday circumstances, and most of us are more like those townsfolk than we are like Jesus or the ancient desert hermits. God comes to us where we are; God is with us in our own lives, in our streets and market squares, wherever we go and whatever we do. We, like our spiritual ancestors, can find inspiration in the words of Psalm 139, from which the title of this book is drawn:

O Lord, you have searched me and known me.
You know when I sit down and when I rise up;
you discern my thoughts from far away.
You search out my path and my lying down,
and are acquainted with all my ways.

Psalm 139:1-3

Staying put can be very challenging; moving on can be easier. But a seed only puts down roots and sprouts once it is embedded in the soil. It is a slow process. It can become complicated as we allow our lives to become entwined, briar-like, with the lives of those around us, accepting the flowers and fruit in their seasons as well as the scratchy thorns. We do not all want that level of intimacy or involvement – entanglement, even. So how do we balance our love of freedom with our adult responsibilities, our sense of loyalty and love towards others, our sense of commitment, our hope that we will find fulfilment in the ordinariness of our lives? Developing discernment about when to stay and when to go is part of the spiritual journey.

Journaling

You might relate this reflection to your initial thoughts about personal perspectives on the Celtic cross, especially the circle element.

Pause and reflect in your journal about the place where you live now. See it as the centre of a circle, widening out from your street to your community, to your wider neighbourhood however you define it, and beyond – city, surrounding countryside . . . You can make this visual by viewing a satellite image of your home on the internet and gradually zooming out. Think about the characters and things that are particular to that place, and how you feel about being there. Why are you there? What is your home like? What is the locality like, from a human perspective – local amenities and so on – and from an earth-centred perspective – hills, valleys, streams, climate, green areas, danger zones. Is it a *safe* place? You might like to add maps or photos to your journal.

When you have done this, read back over your account and think of three words that sum up your place.

Next, think about a place you have been to or know about which is built up around a figure or a spiritual centre. The local town which has grown up around the church and village green will do; alternatively, Iona or Lindisfarne are Celtic examples. You might even have been to Glendalough or another ancient Celtic monastic site. Imagine this place as the centre of a Celtic cross, the community spreading out as the circle. What paths draw you and others in, and what energies leave the place, along the arms of the cross?

Again, when you have written your reflection, read over it and come up with three words to sum up your feelings about this community.

Journaling example

Thinking of a community, I came up with Findhorn. Although it's a long time since I went, it was really important to me. I was only 19 and some Christian friends tried to talk me out of going, but that just made me more determined. I had read about this place where a woman living in a caravan in a gravel park by the sea got messages from God telling her how to grow giant cabbages, and I wanted to see it for myself!

I absolutely loved being there! I'm not sure I'd want to go back, but I was very strongly drawn there. There was a huge pull, and all sorts of strange coincidences fell into place to get me there. That's like one of the arms of the cross – the long one planted in the earth, maybe. I didn't want to leave – the arm going straight back out again. I was really attracted to staying there, but I knew I would be escaping and I had to get on with ordinary life. Life pulled me back out again – relationships, a new term at university . . .

I felt that there was so much love there, it radiated out and lit me up. I was really ready to be lit up. I don't know if that would happen again, but it seemed such a thriving, creative, healing, spiritual place. The gardens were pretty impressive, but there was beautiful growth of human souls going on too.

I don't talk about it much. I found it met with a lot of disapproval by church people who didn't trust it, and thought I was getting lost. This is one of the things that made me move away from the Church: I don't like people trying to control me or make judgements based on ignorance and fear. They need to go and see for themselves! To me, I felt the place gave out a strong sense of openness and a desire to connect lovingly with nature, and I think that's exactly what we need. I know I'm talking about it how it was in the 1980s rather than now, and from my perspective rather than anyone else's, but we do each have to go with what speaks to us, and this was a formative community experience for me.

Three words: love, nature, healing.

Here are three prayers for your home or a place you connect with as your spiritual centre. Choose one or more to add to your journal, changing it if this helps. You could also take some of the six words you singled out and use them in prayer, meditation or creative expression, thinking about what these qualities mean to you.

God bless my home,
wall to wall,
upstairs and down.
God bless the sitting space, the windows for light.
God bless the cooking place, meeting place,
washing place, sleeping place.
God bless this loving place,
from foundation to roof.
God bless all who dwell within,
God bless all who are welcomed in,
and God go with each of us
who cross the threshold,
out into the world
through the open door.
Amen.

Thanks to you, O loving God,
thanks to you for creating this place.
Thanks to you, O roaming Spirit,
thanks to you for bringing me here.
Thanks to you, O companion Christ,
thanks to you for going on ahead.
Here may I bring love,
here may I find love,
here may I stay until a timely day,
here may I stay until it is time to go.
Amen

Peace upon this place,
peace at the heart, peace at the centre.
Peace within this place,
peace at the boundaries, peace at the doors.
Peace be upon this place,
peace at the meeting points, peace in the sharing.
Peace flow in and peace flow out of this place:
a river of peace, bearing blessings;
a river of peace-giving life.
Peace, peace, peace.
Amen

A visual meditation

Go back to the idea of your home being the centre of a circle. During a period of peace, imagine or describe to yourself the concentric rings of your love radiating out further and further. Start with the room you are in, go out to the garden if you have one, your nearest neighbours, then the whole street, including creatures – garden birds, foxes, cats and dogs – and businesses or other work buildings in the street. Go wider and wider, radiating your love out to the whole region, the whole land, until you have encompassed the whole world with your love. You might want to do this over a series of sessions, gradually spreading further out. When you get as far as radiating love to the whole globe, it can be a very powerful experience to do this with a globe in your hands. Love sent out in any direction to travel around the globe comes back to you, of course.

As you do this meditation, notice if there are any places where you come to a barrier and find it difficult to send love. Do not criticise yourself about this; just notice it and take time to think about why this is, what pain you associate with that area. There is no point exercising insincerity, going through the motions of extending love when we do not really mean it, just because we think we ought to. What is worthwhile, however, is recognising inner anger and pain, acknowledging it, being compassionate with ourselves and seeking ways to shift that difficult feeling, because holding on to it is not doing us any good. It can take a lot of digging to get to the bottom of such feelings – we do tend to bury them, especially if we have been creating an impression to the outside world that all is well. It is often worth finding a competent listener who can help us in this process. Include any such thoughts in your journal as an exercise in self-honesty.

Journaling example

Here is an example journal entry from somebody who did the concentric circles of love meditation.

> I lit a candle and calmed my breathing, like when I am going to meditate, then began to visualise my love radiating out. I sent love to my home and garden and to my neighbours and to the local school and shop, and to the shops up the road, and the town, and I imagined zooming out so that I was high up above my home, my arms outstretched to extend love to everyone. I was seeing myself as a bit like an angel – I hope that's not conceited, but it felt good. I was gently rotating, up in the sky, to make sure I reached all around.

Then I started thinking about maps and roads and I noticed the traffic on the roads and my whole mood changed. I didn't feel loving any more. I thought of noise and pollution, and how angry I get as a cyclist that car drivers are so inconsiderate. I started reliving an incident where someone turned right across my path the other day and made me brake really suddenly. I noticed I was judging drivers, getting righteous about the pollution, and 'if I can cycle why can't they?' and getting upset about my near-accident. So. This tells me something: it tells me I have a lot of anger about modern travel and the environment.

Where is the love? I love the environment; I love myself, obviously – I don't want to end up under a bus. I know loads of people who drive, and of course I love of a lot of them and understand why they use cars and vans or whatever. I understand what pressure people are under; I understand how difficult it is, in this fast-paced world, to juggle jobs and children and shopping and caring for relatives and getting a bit of precious leisure time and trying to keep fit . . .

I know it's really hard, and each person has their own story. And I know traffic is a bigger issue than individuals trying to make their lives work. Issues about public transport and nationalisation, and long-term government investments and infrastructure – it goes on and on. It's a political thing, a justice issue.

In my mind I heard myself up on a platform making an impassioned speech. It surprised me how articulate I was and how much conviction I spoke with, and people were listening. I've been thinking about this ever since. I can't exactly run for local mayor or anything, but I might see if I can get involved in some campaigning. I think there's a local group I can link up with which might lead to something . . . it might help me channel my passion in a positive way instead of all this pent-up rage I live with.

Chapter 6
Being in difficult places: the 'desert'

One of the practices common to both the Desert Fathers and Mothers and to Celtic Christian hermits was to seek out challenging environments in which to test or discipline themselves, as well as to experience the awe of being alone with God. The practice reflected the importance of deserts in the Bible, particularly the 40 years of wandering known as the Exodus, experienced by the Hebrew people led out of Egypt by Moses. This was a formative time, as the people gradually deepened their sense of identity in relation to one another and to God. It was a time when they were in God's presence, when their needs were met and their way was indicated, despite the many hardships.

In the Gospels, John the Baptist lived in the desert, and people would go out to him to listen to his teaching. Jesus was often located in the wilderness or the desert, particularly when he prayed alone, and in the account of him being driven into the desert by the Holy Spirit to face a prolonged ordeal of fasting and temptation (Mark 1:12-13; compare with Matthew 4:1-11 and Luke 4:1-13).

The mystics of the Mediterranean region were able to find similarly arid desert environments in Egypt, the Holy Land and Syria. For the Celtic saints, influenced by this lifestyle, 'deserts' were remote places such as dense woodland caves, uninhabited islands or crevices in cliffs, beautiful but incredibly austere – and typically cold and rainy rather than arid!

In terms of our ongoing Celtic cross reflection, it is an interesting question to ask ourselves where we might locate such a desert. Is it the gaps in the quadrants of the circle, where we go off road? Is it the endless space beyond the circle? Or is it one of the paths, the hardest path, perhaps the one heading north, or towards the burning sun? Perhaps we find the desert experience in different locations at different times.

The desert tradition included a strongly ascetic streak of extreme self-denial and endurance of naturally harsh conditions, and also a practice sometimes called 'spiritual warfare': fighting demons. The ascetic developed resilience, flexibility, inner strength, an ability to transcend physical discomfort, and fearlessness, as well as great humility and trust in God. Demons, it was thought, might try to tempt a person off their dedicated path, taunt them with self-doubt, or generally cause them distress – physical, emotional or spiritual. It seems they were especially drawn to holy souls trying to dedicate their lives to God, but the process of facing the demons was a necessary part of the spiritual journey.

Times have changed. Extreme asceticism is definitely a fringe pursuit, and self-mortification is not generally encouraged or viewed as healthy today. There are also mixed opinions about demons. Some prefer a literal approach: demons are described in the Gospels, Jesus came into contact with them, and therefore they must be real. Others prefer a more psychological interpretation: the writers at the time had an ancient worldview that was very different to ours; our spiritual and emotional difficulties are not caused by an enemy spirit 'out there', bent on destroying us, but rather by the complexities and projections of our own unconscious minds, in relation to formative experiences. The path to healing and wholeness is not so much about exorcism but a path of deepening self-understanding and self-forgiveness. Whatever our view, often we find that we still need to face our 'demons', literal or figurative, in order to move on, and it is in the 'desert' places that we notice them most strongly.

Sooner or later, most of us come to a point in our life journey where we enter what we might call a desert. Rather than seeking out such places, we often stumble into them inadvertently. How we respond to our own desert times and what spiritual resources we draw on will depend on our personal circumstances and outlook – and may relate to our personal inclination, as explored in chapter 1. If you are experiencing a difficult time or place right now or are haunted by the memory of difficulties, please consider who or what can give you appropriate support in moving on and processing your experience in a positive way. The exploration of ideas below can only begin to offer general support.

Journaling questions

- What are your thoughts on demons and deserts?

- Where might you locate the desert in relation to the Celtic cross?

- In general, what kind of places make you feel uneasy? What kind of places help you feel safe and relaxed? Or if you prefer, describe a specific place.

Journaling examples

Basically I feel uncomfortable if I'm in a place where it looks as though I could easily be trapped. I have had a couple of nasty experiences, but I'm ok about them now. I've had counselling and this helped me. I also get the creeps around places with a violent history, but I don't know if that is my imagination running riot.

A good illustration of this happened the other Saturday night when I found myself in a part of the city I have never been to before, to meet friends. I knew roughly where it was. It looked ok on the map, but I left a busy street with restaurants and bars, then got to a footbridge over a dual carriageway. The steps up to the bridge involved going round corners and I couldn't see what was round the corner – just concrete and metal posts, then the traffic underneath. I was thinking, 'This is stupid: what if there's someone round the corner?' I could feel my heart starting to beat faster and I was thinking, 'If someone makes a grab at me, where can I run?' Well, there was nobody there, and I crossed over and soon got to the venue, but I definitely felt uncomfortable with the bridge. When I got there, there was a plaque on the wall that said this was the site of the last hanging in the city. I felt quite uncomfortable about that too. I didn't really dwell on it; I just went in and got a drink, but thinking about it now I'm wondering what kind of effect that could have on a place.

Or

Somebody a while back suggested to me that I was being oppressed by evil spirits, because of people I know and things I have done, and that this is why

I sometimes suffer migraines and bouts of depression. I found this unhelpful and was really angry for a long time – it felt as though the person was trying to frighten me into believing in Jesus in order to protect myself spiritually, and trying to stop me respecting the doctors' diagnosis.

I can't be doing with this fear-based kind of religion. I need ways to relax and to feel at peace and am open to exploring how I can find peace through spiritual ways, to help me live with my condition. I think we need to be careful what we say to one another about mental health, whatever we really believe; it's a sensitive issue and people who are ill are very vulnerable.

Christ of peace

We can choose how we read the Gospels. Some like to take them literally, demons and all, as historical accounts (although there are literary and historical challenges with doing this, not least the discrepancies between different Gospel accounts); others prefer to appreciate them as works of literature – story – or as conveyors of allegorical meaning. By reading allegorically we can indeed find many layers of meaning.

One account which has spoken to many who find themselves in a spiritually or an emotionally difficult place is the account in Mark 4:35-41, where Jesus stills a storm on the lake of Galilee in the presence of his terrified disciples. In this account, the challenge to the disciples is not demons but adverse weather, and the location is not a desert but a large lake. For us, this might relate to the lake or sea in some of the inclination pictures in chapter 1.

On that day, when evening had come, he said to them, 'Let us go across to the other side.' And leaving the crowd behind, they took him with them in the boat, just as he was. Other boats were with him. A great gale arose, and the waves beat into the boat, so that the boat was already being swamped. But he was in the stern, asleep on the cushion; and they woke him up and said to him, 'Teacher, do you not care that we are perishing?' He woke up and rebuked the wind, and said to the sea, 'Peace! Be still!' Then the wind ceased, and there was a dead calm. He said to them, 'Why are you afraid? Have you still no faith?' And they were filled with great awe and said to one another, 'Who then is this, that even the wind and the sea obey him?'

Mark 4:35-41

Water is often a symbol of our own unconscious, and storms on a lake or at sea can represent our inner torments. The sea can represent our 'desert' experiences of fear and confusion, the difficulty we have in understanding what is going on and our struggle to gain control of our lives. The story above can be seen as describing Christ in our boat at such times of crisis – along with companions.

In the Christian faith, especially the Celtic Christian faith, there is a very strong tradition of Christ's strong companionship and the protective power of prayer, including that of a loving community, which can support any journey into our own inner troubles, by sea or by land. We will think more about this spiritual community soon.[3]

---

3. For an extended meditation on this boat image, see page 150 in my book, *Hiding in God: Reflecting on personal health concerns through prayer* (Buxhall: Kevin Mayhew, 2012).

An alternative biblical image in which many have found comfort over the centuries, when faced with a difficult path, is that of the caring Shepherd. Psalm 23 expresses the sense of safety in walking with God, our shepherd. In Christian thinking, Jesus is also known as the Good Shepherd, drawing on a parable attributed to Jesus in which he describes a shepherd going to search for a lost sheep and celebrating when it is found (Luke 15:3-7).[4]

> The Lord is my shepherd, I shall not want.
> He makes me lie down in green pastures;
> he leads me beside still waters;
> he restores my soul.
> He leads me in right paths
> for his name's sake.
> Even though I walk through the darkest valley,
> I fear no evil;
> for you are with me;
> your rod and your staff –
> they comfort me.
>
> *Psalm 23:1-4*

A strong biblical impression, whether we prefer to think about desert, lake or a rough path through a gloomy valley, is of God's companionship with us. Much of our pain might be attributed to difficulty in feeling the divine presence, yet with hindsight, these challenging periods are often important in our development and can be spiritually rich. Having said that, we are our own best judges on this issue; some experiences are quite simply destructive and it would

---

4. For an extended reflection on the metaphor of the Good Shepherd, see my book, *Rejoice with Me: Hope for lost sheep* (Buxhall: Kevin Mayhew, 2013).

be better never to have had them, no matter what others say. Seeking healing from such experiences, an end to the pain they have caused, requires time and appropriate support.

Journaling again

- Taking the story of Jesus stilling the storm as allegorically as you like, reflect on how it makes you feel, what the storm might represent to you, who is in your boat with you. What or who, to you, is a source of calm?

- What are your feelings about Psalm 23 and the metaphor of God as a caring shepherd guiding you through difficulties?

Resources for the desert

Here are two prayers, should you wish to use them:

I appeal to the Most High,
Son of Mary and Spirit of Truth,
to aid me in my distress, on sea and on land.
May the Three strengthen me,
may the Three shield me,
may the Three watch over me
by day and by night.
May God bring me to safety,
may God hold me,
may God protect me,
now and always.
Amen

Relieve me, O God,
of my suffering,
for I am torn by a burden
that will not let me go;
like an anchor caught in weeds, it pulls,
and my boat goes round in circles.
I am helpless to move on,
afraid of being dragged down.
O Love of loves and Chief of chiefs,
O God of grace and mercy,
relieve me of my suffering
and set me free
to live the life of gladness,
to live the life of trust in you.
Amen

Protective place and person prayers: the caim

One of the most well-known prayer types of Celtic tradition is the caim, which is uttered while describing a protective circle around oneself. You can imagine yourself standing at the centre of the Celtic cross, drawing that wide circle around you with a ring of light, or perhaps a stream of living water so that you are safe on your island of four quarters. There are long caims and short ones; to me, they work best if recited off by heart, so rhythm and rhyme help.

Here is one; you might enjoy crafting your own:

Holy One and Holy Three,
ever-blessed Trinity,
encircle me all round about,
let only love come in or out!
Amen

There is also the tradition of the *lorica*, a 'breastplate' or armour prayer, the most well-known of which is the *lorica* of St Patrick, otherwise known as the 'Cry of the deer'. There are several versions of this, all widely available, including in hymn form. The following is a contemporary version respecting gender equality which I wrote for use as a chant (with a little practice), with a drum if you like.

St Patrick's Breastplate

I arise today [or: I lie down tonight]
through a mighty strength,
the invocation of the Trinity,
through belief in the Threeness,
through confession of the oneness
of the Creator-Creatrix of all creation.

I arise today
through the strength of Christ's birth
and the power of his baptism,
through the strength of his crucifixion
and the power of his burial,
through the strength of his resurrection
and the power of his ascension,
through the strength of his descent for the comfort of all.
I arise today
through the love of the cherubim,
the obedience of angels,
the service of archangels,
in hope of resurrection, to meet with blessing,
in the ancient prayers of our ancestors in faith,
in prophets' preaching,

in apostles' surrender,
in faith of confessors,
in devotion of lovers,
in deeds of mercy and compassion.

I arise today
through the strength of heaven:
light of sun
and radiance of moon,
splendour of fire
and speed of lightning,
swiftness of wind
and depth of sea,
stability of earth
and firmness of rock.

I arise today
through God's strength to lead me,
God's might to uphold me,
God's wisdom to guide me,
God's eye to look before me,
God's ear to hear me,
God's word to speak for me,
God's hand to guard me,
God's way to lie before me,
God's shield to protect me,
God's host to save me
from snares and mischief,
from temptations of vices,
and from any being
who might wish me ill,

afar and near,
alone and in multitude.
I trust today each one of these powers,
between me and any form of harm,
against any force that may wish me ill,
against misleading messengers,
against loveless laws,
against ignorance of fools,
against empty idolatry,
against violence and fear,
against everything that harms any child of God.

Christ to shield me through day and night
against venom, against burning,
against drowning, against wounding,
so that I may enjoy abundance of blessings.

Christ be with me, Christ before me,
Christ behind me, Christ within me,
Christ beneath me, Christ above me,
Christ on my right, and Christ on my left,
Christ when I lie down,
Christ when I sit down,
Christ when I arise and when I sleep,
Christ in the heart of all who think of me,
Christ in the mouth of all who speak of me,
Christ in every eye that sees me,
Christ in every ear that hears me,
Christ be all and all be Christ.
Amen

Journaling

We have covered quite a lot of ground in this last section, even though we have largely been reflecting on staying put in one place. In your journal, if you haven't already, write about your reaction to anything that has come up in this section, positive or negative. Whether your opinion is that spiritual warfare is an unhelpful concept, or that spiritual protection is the most important aspect of Celtic spirituality, write about it!

Especially:

- Do you find yourself more drawn to the idea of a gloomy valley, a desert or the sea to describe your challenging times? Are you more drawn to the idea of demonic entities or to amoral natural phenomena, such as storms, to describe your inner troubles?

- If there is a prayer, a story or a passage of Scripture that appeals to you, consider reflecting further on it, perhaps through other media such as song, artwork or dance.

Journaling examples

There's a shop doorway where a homeless person was attacked and died of injuries. We heard about it in our house group and decided to go there and say some prayers. To start with we prayed for him, then we prayed for the attacker. Then we were quiet for a bit, and then someone prayed for the town, and what it is, that people are homeless anyway, and someone prayed for the police, and the families of everyone, then we prayed for the shop and its owners and the customers. We asked for God's Spirit of healing on everything and everyone and lit some tea lights.

While we were lighting the candles, passers-by stopped and wanted to know what we were doing, so we told them. They stood around for a bit. The next day I went by and there was a bunch of flowers there, and soon after there were quite a few bunches. I think we did something lovely, not just for the man who died but also for the locals, helping them deal with violence and death lovingly.

Or

We have to face facts; there's not a lot of point getting all emotional and worrying about spiritual powers when we don't have enough information. Better to stay in the real world. There's more to be concerned about in the problems of the world. Poverty scares me, pensions, child malnutrition, climate change, the injustices that are going on all around us . . . these are the things that haunt me, and there's no doubt they are real. I'm scared about the rise of fascism, what happens when people start demonising other groups, blaming others for society's problems instead of looking deeper at our own prejudices. What's the world going to be like when my grandchildren are grown up? That scares me.

Part 3

Who is with me?

Chapter 7
Soul friends and networks of love

In this chapter we begin to think about who is with us on the journey.

We are linked into large networks of other human beings in which there is constant exchange in practical, emotional and spiritual ways. This connection is added to by the many one-way influences we experience through the media, entertainers and so on, as we are moved in different ways by people 'out there' who do not know us.

Even when we are alone, we remain connected to others, however remotely. The book we are reading links us to the author. The radio links us to the presenters and their hosts, and to the musicians. The letters we receive are delivered by someone who comes to our home, and sent by a person who, for a while, perhaps thought about our name, our concern. We belong to multiple communities, whether we have consciously opted into them or not, and we play a part, giving and receiving. Even a stay in hospital is the entry into a community for a while; passing through an airport, we trust ourselves to a community of people. When shopping, we enter the community of the shop, its suppliers, the producers, the fellow customers and team of sales assistants.

We could draw each of the links we have to other people as a network of lines, spreading out in ever increasing circles. The lines are not always love lines. But the more we reflect on interconnectedness, and on the cross underlying the circle, the more we can increase the energy of love circulating in our lives, because the centre of the cross, for a Christian, always leads back to Christ. For people on a Christian faith path, even when they are alone in the eyes of the world, it can be a comfort to reflect on the companionship of Jesus and 'all the company of heaven' referred to in liturgy. There are networks at many levels.

Intercessions in a church group or in private sometimes have the effect of defining these networks of love, helping us to reach out to others beyond us, to acknowledge that they matter, to us and to God, and to take the time to pray for them. People on the other side of the world can be brought close and transformed from nameless 'nobodies' to cherished individuals, through thoughtful prayer.

Journaling activity

This activity relates to the initial reflection about personal perspectives on the Celtic cross, emphasising the importance of the circular element and the way the cross can relate to the circle. The circle is especially about outreach and community, the groups we are part of. In the inclinations in chapter 1, the circle is represented by the idea of a village.

(If this is used as part of a group activity, it needs to be presented with sensitivity, respecting people's privacy regarding their personal relationships. Represent people with symbols rather than names, and do not ask participants to share anything other than what they volunteer freely.)

Pause to think about the people in your life. Sketch a large Celtic cross, but rather than drawing just one circle, draw concentric circles spreading outwards from the centre, each one larger than the one before. Write 'Me' at the centre. You may feel that this seems egocentric, but as the exercise is about your own personal network of connections it makes sense to put you at the hub of it. It may also seem appropriate to acknowledge Christ at the centre of the cross somehow, or permeating the whole thing. (You might prefer to represent your thoughts using string and buttons, marbles or pebbles for different people – even a dartboard laid flat and different coloured drawing pins will do – then take a photo of it for your journal.)

When you have 'centred' yourself and thought about how you wish to represent the divine presence in your life, go on to consider who is closest to the centre – those who know or knew you best and have the most influence in your life. This may be a partner or parents, perhaps a brother or sister or a group of close friends. It is for you to decide how much of a space you leave between yourself and others.

If it seems appropriate to pause and pray, to light a candle or to do something that helps you to acknowledge your feelings at this point, please do so.

When you are ready, and this may be days or weeks later if necessary, consider the next circles, as they spread out. Think about other people in your life, and how close or distant you might place them in relation to yourself. You can use the four arms of the cross to divide your relationships into family, friends, work colleagues and church community, or some other meaningful arrangement that suits your circumstances (boundaries will blur!). You can include those with who you are in conflict or who have a negative influence as well as those you get on well with: people from the past; people who come into your life briefly then go again, from solicitors to shop assistants; members of groups you belong to, including social media networks; even groups of people such as a class of children or a sports team that you support.

Include on the diagram the names of any who have inspired and supported your journey along the way, or who have just appreciated you for who you are. You might find that you have been most inspired by an elderly aunt or a shop steward at work, or a teacher, or a neighbour, maybe someone from another faith, or someone with no apparent religion at all.

When you feel that you have finished, take time to look at your diagram. Threads may start to emerge, linking different people. Draw these connections in. Your circles may start to look like a spider's web hanging from the cross. There will be love in the web, but other emotions, too. Try to name these: confusion, grief, frustration, bitterness, loyalty, disappointment, attraction, concern, guilt, anger, gratitude . . . ?

- Which emotions seem to come up most often?

- Where are the happier feelings?

- Where are the more challenging feelings?

- Where are the particularly influential characters, for good or ill?

As you reflect on these relationships, think about how you might use the diagram to support your prayers – and how your prayers might support your own resolution of feelings and issues. With this reflection focusing on relationships and emotions, it is natural for unresolved feelings to come up. If this is the case, it is worth considering talking to an experienced listener for support.

The prayer included here is for optional use, or you can choose one from a different source to add to your journal. Continue to meditate on your diagram and all that it tells you in whatever way helps you: there is no rush; something might occur to you weeks later.

Christ at my centre,
Christ all around me,
encompass the whole wide circle of my dear ones,
encompass all those I must learn to love;
encompass especially, [Name], your own dear one
in your own good time
and in your own true way,
O Christ of the cross,
O Christ of the people,
O Christ of the mantle of love.
Amen

Journaling examples

I drew my cross and circles radiating out. It felt strange to put myself at the centre, with Christ there on the cross, but if Christ is with me or within me, then it seems good to put us together. Putting myself on the cross seemed like a statement of faith, a recognition that God permeates all my relationships. For a moment the cross and concentric circles looked like the sights of a camera – I felt the focus fall on me. I felt the truth of that verse in Psalm 139: 'You have searched me and known me.' And God knows every single person I have written on my plan, and everyone beyond it too. There's great wonder in that, for me.

Or

I put my wife at the centre with me: nobody could possibly know me better than she does. Her love is often how I feel God's love is getting through to me, with her patience and the way nothing is too much trouble. I put Jeanie (my ex) further out, with a movement line to show she used to be close to my centre as well. But I don't think she was ever quite as close as Bel and I are now. We were friends, and then we just didn't 'get' each other any more. We saw life so differently, wanted such different things.

I drew the children quite close to me, but they are grown up now. Angie is the closest; the boys are a bit further out, but there's a strong bond between us really. And of course there are bonds with their mum, and with Bel, too. And they have bonds between each other, too. I drew all these connections. It matters a lot to me that they love each other and support each other.

The work colleagues are all further out – we keep a professional distance: all except Hugh – we've known each other so long he's definitely a friend I trust. I wrote his name on the line between friends and work colleagues, and then noticed what a place of strength this seems to be – an arm of the cross. He is a strength to me.

Or

The first part made me feel very sad and I wanted to run away from it. In fact, when we began it in the group I left the room and went and had a good cry. To start with it was anger as much as sadness – I hadn't come along to be made to feel miserable, or to embarrass myself in front of everyone by crying. That wore off after a bit and I just felt very lonely. Whenever I say to myself, 'I'm so lonely,' it brings up a big well of emotion and sets me off crying. I wanted to be able to say it to someone; I wanted someone to hear it, and the fact that I was outside on my own added to my feeling of isolation. But then one of the others came out to check I was OK and I found it really easy to just say the words. I felt heard. There was no attempt to solve my problems or trivialise my experience – just a feeling of being heard. There's God in that listening, for me. It's still true that I'm lonely, but it seems to be held somehow now, and I have some hope that God's going to help me through it, whereas before I wasn't sure God even knew or cared.

The communion of the saints

The 'communion of saints' is an expression found in the Apostles' Creed. It describes the spiritual community of the body of Christ – those who are 'in communion' or who share the faith. The Church is a vast body, stretching back 2000 years, with many different denominations exploring different ways of practising Christianity. Those who follow Jesus find their own places of belonging within the whole. There is difference and diversity, just as there are points of shared identity.

Among the people we walk with on our life path, sometimes someone stands out as particularly loving, inspiring or wise, and we find that in their presence we feel safe exploring the questions at our heart about life's meaning and purpose. They are good listeners, and their rich personal experience adds to their capacity to listen with humility. We might think of such people as soul friends, or *anamchara*. Among the saints we are going to think about below, many, if not all, acted as soul friends to others and had soul friends themselves, and many, such as Ita, advised their students that to have a soul friend is one of life's necessities.

There is a sense of this loving connection, or communion with saints, in a great many of the prayers from Celtic sources. Disciples, angels and holy people of local renown are spoken of fondly as though present or hastening to be present with people in everyday life, to stand alongside earthly people, whether to help them with their work, to protect them at night or to be there at the bedside with loving relatives, in sickness or childbirth. The impression of safe, loving proximity suggests 'thinness', a feeling that there is a spiritual presence in everyday life which is almost tangible, just beyond a veil. The linear concept of passing time dissolves so that past, present and even future can somehow meet. For some, this connection is about discovering roots or spiritual ancestors who can help us in our search for identity and meaning.

Chief of chiefs in the spiritual community of Christians is Jesus. An image that shines out from the illustrated manuscripts of the Celtic Church is of a Jesus who has been embraced by the prevalent northern European culture of the day and represented as one of 'them', complete with blond curls and fair skin. While cultures around the world have represented Jesus as belonging to their own people, it is equally important today, given Christianity's catastrophic history of anti-Semitism and, from the West at least, cultural imperialism, to remember that Jesus was an Eastern-Mediterranean Jew of the first century, to be respectful of his roots and the (continuing) faith of Judaism, and to be clear about celebrating the diversity of cultural heritage that makes up our society today.

While we are about to engage with 16 characters mainly from the British Isles, their stories are not unlike the stories of spiritually minded, creation-loving people around the world and from the Bible. It would be an interesting exercise to draw in other characters to replace or supplement the list offered here, to add a sense of global community, for contemporary 'Celtic' Christianity to be a way forward in creative living today rather than a question of heritage or an excuse for tribalism.

While the holy people of the Celtic tradition have come to be called 'saints', most of them are not officially canonised. St Patrick, St David, St Brigid – the 'big' names – are 'proper' saints, but for the most part, 'saint' is meant in the sense of an ordinary person dedicated to God and leading an extraordinary life because of it. There is a great deal of material about some of the better-known saints, who had 'lives' or reverential biographies written about them for the edification of the faithful, although many of the stories stayed quite local to the characters themselves until the hunger for folklore led collectors of the eighteenth and nineteenth centuries to seek them out. Such accounts date back more than a thousand years and were written some time after the death of the people in question. This means we are not dealing with historical accounts as we like to think of them today.

The augmentation of wonders and the diminishing of personal weakness is part of the storytelling tradition of legend. This we know from contemporary caricatures of 'fishermen's tales', where an average-sized catch turns in the telling to a larger and larger fish until the story becomes incredible. Such stories begin with real people and events, but over the years details are shaped a little, embellishments are added, details are left out, new accounts about other people are woven in and time frames are squeezed and stretched so that, for example, it becomes possible to contemplate St Brigid acting as midwife to Mary even though Brigid lived in fifth-century Ireland. For those who wish to adhere to literal facts, such play with the passage of time is frustrating, yet what matters in the story is the symbolic value of nursing the baby Jesus, and of being a character so caring and thoughtful that she really would make the long journey into a strange land to help a young family in need, and she really would be a blessing to have at the bedside for any labouring mother. Equally important is the weaving in – as with Joseph of Arimathea – of the lives and experiences of people from the British Isles with the life of Jesus. Taking the gospel as their own, they crossed boundaries of time and space to draw closer and enter into the immediacy of the biblical narratives. Those of us who practise Ignatian contemplation or guided visualisation on passages of the Bible do something similar, imagining ourselves into the descriptions that seem so alive to us.

Another aspect of ancient legends that can be a challenge to modern readers with a penchant for the literal is the delight in mythical beasts and wondrous works, miraculous or magical. In days gone by, such tales (as with young children even now) could more easily evoke a simple sense of wonder, whereas our increased knowledge today can lead to the idea that they are impossible, fanciful, ridiculous, wrong and therefore not the 'truth', not worth bothering with. Yet, as stories, they can continue to hold meaning and value.

So I invite you to enter into the allegorical when reading of St Patrick turning himself into a deer with a charm, or St Columba banishing the Loch Ness monster, or Ia sailing over the sea on a leaf – as one might when reading of Jesus walking on the water or feeding five thousand from a basket of five loaves and two fish.

Journaling

Before you begin reading about the different characters, pause to think about what the 'communion of the saints' and the idea of 'holiness' mean to you.

Journaling examples

I have no roots in the British Isles and no particular attachment to its ancient places, although the idea of thinness interests me and I feel it in some of my own favourite places. So I am pleased to be invited to bring characters from my own culture into the circle of friends, as I see it. I have begun thinking about who I could include, from those known personally to me and my family to people in our history. The idea is something like respecting ancestors, which is very important. It's not worshipping them, but it is honouring the dignity and struggle of their lives and the gift of life that they have passed down to us. As I carry the genes of my flesh-and-blood ancestors and live out a future for them that they could not imagine, I feel a connection and a respect for the continuity of life over the generations. It makes me think I will be the ancestor of somebody one day, and I wonder what stories they will tell about me.

Holiness is about God breaking through in lives. Because people open up and let God in, they shine and people can't help but notice that they are shining, but it is God's glory, not their own. When you meet a shining person you know they are special; you don't forget them. I'm trying to think of people like that.

Or

Sharing Communion at the Abbey, I felt so lifted up; it was joyous. The place is so old – I don't know a great deal about the history, but that didn't matter – I could feel the prayerfulness in the atmosphere. It was a stillness lit by sunbeams pouring through the little windows up above the pillars, and the dust sparkled. I was sitting in a worn old pew where I could imagine so many worshippers sitting before, singing, chanting, praying, loving. The seat itself felt powerful, a place where I knew my brothers and sisters in faith had left a prayerful memory in the wood itself. I reached out to touch the shelf in front of me, where I had put my hymn book, to touch what they had touched. Walking up the nave to the altar, it was as though I was part of a long, long line of people stretching way back in time, and kneeling at the altar, my eyes closed, it was as though they were kneeling with me. How many have drunk from that cup? We are all one . . .

Engaging with the saints

Below are 16 characters – eight women and eight men – who are members of the Celtic Christian community and to whom we might turn for loving or inspiring companionship.

I have described key aspects of their lives, but there are more stories to be found about many of these Celtic saints, and there are also different versions of some of the stories – as is the nature of legends retold over the years. Please do supplement the summaries I have given with your own information, especially if I have missed out your favourite stories. I have also suggested key symbols traditionally associated with them, or which we could associate with them, but be creative and see if any symbols or associations come up that work better for you personally. Rather than writing prayers to them, I have modelled simple letters – emails if you prefer – as though seeking to get in touch as one might with a real live spiritual accompanier.

- Read the descriptions one by one. Take as much time as you like – you could spend a day or more with each character over an extended period, even, while you continue with the book if you are concerned about losing pace.

- Find out more, paint, draw, sing, dance their lives – get to know them!

- As I suggested earlier, think about bringing in new characters from further afield who resonate with the same spirit, as you see it.

- Reflect on the suggested qualities and how these resonate with you. Add to the list if you want to. Reflect also on aspects that you find challenging, and why. This is not about being judgemental, but about giving space for your own perspective. It is only natural to warm to some and feel uncomfortable with others, as in real life. You might feel that some characters relate quite well to one or more of the eight inclinations described in chapter 1.

- Think about how you might talk with them or be with them, if they were part of your circle of acquaintances. What might you write, if you wanted to get in touch? How might they respond?

Joseph of Arimathea, first century AD

Joseph of Arimathea is not indigenous to 'Celtic' culture. In the Gospels he is named as a member of the Jewish council in Jerusalem at the time of Jesus' execution, and he obtained permission to remove Jesus' corpse from the cross in order to pay his respects by offering a dignified burial in his own tomb. As the Gospels tell us, Joseph was accompanied by Jesus' women followers, who witnessed the burial. It seems they trusted him, and it is possible that the women knew him, since they were not against him taking the body or afraid to go with him at such a moment of crisis.

According to medieval legend, Joseph was a tin trader who travelled to Cornwall by ship to collect supplies, which he brought back to ports in the Holy Land. Cornwall's tin mines were a well-kept secret in the ancient world. He was also, according to the same legend, Jesus' uncle, and some say he brought the young Jesus with him to the British Isles.

It is said that Joseph travelled up from Cornwall to Glastonbury, which in those days was a hill surrounded by marshy land, and an ancient centre of farming and orchards, learning and spiritual practice. Here, Joseph struck his staff into the ground, and like Aaron's staff in the biblical account, the stake burst into flower and took root, becoming the Glastonbury thorn – a species of hawthorn that flowers in the winter. Glastonbury was claimed, because of Joseph's legendary visit, to have been the earliest centre of Christian faith and practice, not only in England but in Europe. This claim helped the Church in later centuries (but not in Celtic times) to argue its rightful independence from the control of Rome.

The idea of Joseph's tin-trade visits, which has entered into popular folklore, weaves together the Celtic connection through Cornwall, the ancient significance of Glastonbury, beloved of many today exploring creative expressions of spirituality, and the rightful place of Judaism in the Christian story.

Joseph of Arimathea is very welcome in the British Isles and reminds us of the heritage of Jesus. He reminds us that, just as Joseph gave Jesus full respect, we are to give Joseph's people full respect too.

Qualities

Respect, courage, authority, generosity, openness, adventure, depth of spirituality.

A letter

Dear St Joseph

First, I want to say sorry. I don't know many Jewish people personally, but I know they are your own people, and Jesus' own people too. It's really awful, what has happened over the centuries since Jesus lived. I want to try to understand what went wrong between Jews and Christians and how we can relearn to love and understand, and heal things in some way. I'd like to hear what you've got to say on that. I feel that I can warm to you – you seem very approachable, bold enough to go and speak to Pilate, kind enough to

*include the women in the procession to the tomb . . .
but I like the idea that you were a tin trader, too – it
somehow roots you in reality, even if it's just a myth. I'd
be very glad to meet with you, maybe even in
Glastonbury itself, or by a flowering hawthorn.
In a spirit of reconciliation,
a fellow elder*

Brigid of Kildare, 451–525 AD

Brigid (or Brigit) is a very rich character with a substantial
body of legend attached to her, so this description can only
offer an overview. If you feel especially drawn to Brigid there
is no end to where your research might take you!

She is full of kindly concern for all, from Mary and the
newborn Jesus, for whom, according to legend, she
(anachronistically) acted as midwife, to a stray dog at the
door. Whatever their need, she would find a way to help
them there and then. Sometimes she was so moved that she
gave away other people's wealth without asking – her (druid)
father's sword, the butter in the dairy, the meat meant for
guests – she so valued each child of God and had such little
value for material things. This impetuousness or impulsive
unilateral action would annoy people, especially those who
owned whatever was given, but it is difficult to fault her
motives. Brigid challenged ideas of ownership and
demonstrated the kingdom value of redistribution to ensure
everyone had enough. Divine abundance rushed to fill the
deficits she created: often, God replaced what she gave away.
She had great confidence in God's free abundance and gave
others reason to have confidence too.

When Brigid came to be admitted to holy orders, it is said
that the presiding bishop spontaneously and inexplicably

used the words of consecration of a bishop, so she was, in a sense, the first woman bishop. Brigid had a fiery love, and kept a fire burning continually at her monastery at Kildare, tended by a group of women. Although the monastery was for men and women, guarding the flame was a role for women only.

Brigid shares the name and many of the attributes of an older character, a deity by the same name. She is associated among other things with fire and milk, whether from domestic creatures or human mothers, and with a bishop's crook. She has her own cross, which she is said to have woven out of straw at a dying man's bedside. It normally has four equal arms, but there are also versions with three arms to symbolise the Trinity.

Qualities

Generosity, compassion, spontaneity, love, lack of materialism, great faith in God's abundance, a sense of freedom, valuing the intrinsic worth of each human being and creature.

A letter

Dear St Brigid

If I am honest, I find your generosity quite unnerving, and I'm a little apprehensive about getting too involved in case you challenge me to give away more than I want to. I feel rather like that about Jesus, too, which makes me understand something of why you are called a saint. You seem so kind, though, that I am drawn to you despite my concerns. You challenge me to be more kind, too, not just to people but to creatures, to all God's children. But I am especially intrigued by the flame you

had burning that was tended by 19 women. I would love to know what that represented for you. To me, it feels like an impressive expression of the Feminine Divine that you would not allow to go out, even in that very male-dominated world. I'd be glad if we could talk together about this. I'd also be honoured to see you as my spiritual bishop and mentor on the Way.
Yours in the fire of love,
a little sister

Patrick, 387–461 AD

Patrick, now the patron saint of Ireland, was kidnapped from a Christian household in south-west Scotland as a youth and taken into slavery in Ireland. He was put to work herding animals and found strength in his faith, his prayers helping him endure harsh outdoor conditions and long nights. Eventually he managed to escape and return home.

Although his parents begged him to stay, Patrick, in response to a dream in which the people of Ireland called to him, decided to go back to Ireland as a missionary. He did not go straight there, but travelled first to France where he studied. When he was ordained bishop, he then returned to the area where he had been kept as a slave. He spent the rest of his life in Ireland and is attributed with converting a large number to Christianity.

Patrick does not seem to have had an easy relationship with pagan leaders of the day, both having a rather confrontational approach to engagement. Patrick is attributed with as many – if not more – acts of strange and sometimes alarming spiritual power as the druids with whom he contended for spiritual authority. There is something reminiscent of the biblical accounts of Elijah in conflict with the prophets of Baal, where contests and demonstrations of power sometimes resulted in injury and even death in the struggle between the faiths. On one occasion, however, rather than engage in spiritual warfare, he recited a charm prayer and turned himself and his companion into deer to evade danger. This is the *lorica*, or the 'Cry of the deer'.

One of Patrick's most famous acts of power is said to be the expulsion of snakes from Ireland, and his most famous teaching is the employment of a three-lobed shamrock leaf to illustrate the concept of the Holy Trinity.

Qualities

Energy, determination, courage, vision, confidence of faith, compassion for the oppressed, spiritual power, teaching.

A letter

Dear St Patrick

I am aware that you are really well known and people hold you in a great deal of respect, so it is with some trepidation that I write. I am not sure I feel comfortable about everything I have heard about you. I've met some really lovely modern-day druids and, while I'm sure they are not like the ones you were up against, I'm also not sure you needed to get as aggressive as you did – allegedly. I thought Christianity was about gentleness and love, not blasting people who don't agree with you. It seems like misuse of spiritual gifts, to me. Having said that, the prayer you wrote, which turned you into a deer – or so they say – is one that I have often reflected on and come back to. I have even written a contemporary version – I hope you don't mind. I want to thank you for that, and for being someone who knew how to disappear as a deer with an incantation, in the name of Christ. That's quite helpful in my dialogue with people today who are exploring earth-centred spiritualities. I would like to talk with you about this aspect of your spirituality – including whether there was something special about deer for you – and I would be very interested to hear what the pagan religion was really like all that time ago so I can form my own opinions. I know you are – or were – a bit biased, but perhaps you have mellowed over the years and are prepared to give a balanced picture.

With respect,
a spiritual seeker hoping for honest dialogue

Non, fifth to sixth century AD

Non chose to commit herself to a quiet life minding her own business in a convent in Pembrokeshire, South Wales, but was noticed by a visiting personage who somehow gained access to her and made her pregnant. Most likely, in the circumstances, she was raped, although there are versions which suggest a more willing liaison. During her pregnancy she was excluded from the convent and from church and not supported by the father of the child. Although she crept into church to listen to a preacher, he somehow sensed she was there and felt unable to speak until she left. This is reported either as a moral judgement on her unmarried pregnancy or a premonition of the holiness of her unborn child.

Non gave birth alone on top of a cliff in a storm – a terrible ordeal – but it is said that light shone around her, and a stone she leaned on bears her handprint to this day. Nearby, a holy spring appeared, which became a place of healing and pilgrimage. She named her child David, and he became the patron saint of Wales. Non brought David up until he reached a suitable age, then, as was quite normal in those days, she fostered him to a monastery where he would receive his education and religious training. Only then did Non return to her own vocation as a nun, travelling by sea to Cornwall and Brittany where she founded several monasteries. She is buried in Brittany.

In Non we find someone who endured complication, disruption and quite likely violation from someone who then walked away unaffected. Her whole life was affected: she suffered exclusion from a community to which she belonged and endured unassisted labour in frightening circumstances. Yet she was also blessed: the storm did not touch her, the child was well cared for, and she went on to live a creative and empowered life. Non suffered but was capable of great forgiveness and generosity of spirit – otherwise she would not have re-entered the convent and become a missionary. She was secure in God's love. A symbol for her could be a stone with a handprint.

Qualities

A sense of self-worth no matter what, courage, inner strength, resilience, integrity, sense of responsibility towards her child whom she 'let go' as a child of God, vision and ability to gain wisdom from adversity, which she turned into service to others.

A letter

Dear St Non

I found your story extremely inspiring. I visited your chapel and shrine on holiday in Wales once, but did not really know much about your life at the time. I really wish I had put more thought into being there. I do remember it was a beautiful stretch of coastline, but I shudder to imagine you up there on the cliffs, giving birth in a storm. I hope I will be able to go back one day and perhaps collect a little water from the well. I like the idea of holy water: I have some on my shrine at home, where I light a candle in front of an icon of Mary and baby Jesus. It reminds me of my baptism, the ideals of my faith.

Like you, I have had quite a difficult life, but I think I have found it more difficult to let go of my sorrows than you did. I would really appreciate being able to share some of the things that have happened to me because I have a feeling you would be able to help me move on and find some peace and wisdom out of it all. I know I need to do this in order to be of more use to others and less self-absorbed, but it's very difficult. If you do not have time, I understand, but perhaps you will at least be able to pray for my healing.

With thanks,

a troubled soul

Columba, 521–597 AD

Columba (in Irish, Columcille) was of Irish royal blood and had significant influence in his homeland, where he was ordained a priest. Legend has it that a dispute broke out over ownership of a copy of a book of psalms he had made. The dispute led to war with the owner of the original manuscript, people lost their lives and Columba went into exile, over the sea to the Scottish island of Iona. He missed Ireland all his life, its people and the oaks.

On Iona, Columba established a spiritual community that had huge influence, from where the gospel gradually spread out across Scotland. Columba seems to have been gifted as a diplomat and won the respect of Pictish leaders, even where he was unable to win converts to Christ. Perhaps his earlier experience of conflict had inspired him to find more peaceable ways to resolve differences.

Columba is attributed with the gift of prophetic insight, including the knowledge of his own impending death, and many miracles, including healings. One legend connects him with a water monster in the river Ness, near the Loch, which he ordered to keep away from a person in the water. He was also said to be able to calm storms and return spilt milk to the pail. Although a person of significant stature, in more ways than one, Columba had a reputation for gentleness and great asceticism. He used to say that deep prayer brought one to tears.

He had a long and influential life, perhaps one in which we might see change, from the mindset of a youthful warrior prince to the wise, dignified humility of a respected sage. He is attributed with saying, among other things, that Jesus was his druid. As he drew close to death, it is said that an elderly white horse came and nuzzled him, with tearful eyes, in farewell. We might associate him with this horse, or the book of psalms, perhaps even a subdued water monster or the oak trees of home that he missed so such.

Qualities

Love of the psalms and prayer, humility, diplomacy, asceticism, integrity, spiritual gifts of healing and prophecy.

A letter

Dear St Columba

I confess I am a little in awe of you – you seem like a larger-than-life personality and I'm not sure you would have much interest in me. I feel rather inadequate in comparison. However, what brings me to write is that I am very drawn by the way you turned a negative like being exiled into such a positive. You turned your experience of a fatal conflict into a lesson in diplomacy and peaceful negotiation. You started off making a secret copy of the psalms because you loved them and wanted them, but ended up sharing the faith with hundreds – thousands. You seem such a positive force. I think that by walking with you, even just a little way, I might pick up some of your energy and your ability to turn things around for good. That's a gift I could really use in my life, if you could make room for me at all.

Yours in hope,

a follower of Christ

Melangell, sixth century AD

Melangell had her life mapped out for her by her parents but she refused to comply with the marriage they had arranged, having given her life to God. She ran away to the Irish coast and travelled by boat to Wales, somehow protected from harm even though she was a solitary young woman.

Melangell carried on inland some distance and then sheltered in a wooded valley, where she became known to the villagers who gave her food and where she spent long hours praying.

One day a hare fleeing a hunting party hid under her cloak. She refused to be intimidated by the dogs and hunters and the leader, a prince, was impressed by her prayerfulness and the hare's refuge with her. He dedicated the land as an area where no creatures would be hunted – an early nature reserve – and gave it to her. Melangell stayed in the area, supported by the locals, and drew others to share her life of prayer, becoming the abbess of a convent. There is still a centre of prayer at her shrine to this day, which has a focus on well-being and prayers for healing. It welcomes people of all faiths and none.

Melangell had courage and a sense of independence, and was confident that she had the right to decide her own life, her faith and how she spent her time. She was confident enough in God to travel alone and to stand her ground in the face of an aggressor. Nobody hurt her – rather, they welcomed her prayers for them, and by her presence she gave refuge to a frightened creature and converted a prince away from violence towards peace. She was a seemingly vulnerable woman, yet somehow was surrounded by a protective shield of peace.

Her symbol is usually a hare, but could also be a cloak, the mantle of protection for all seeking refuge.

Qualities

Prayerfulness, solitude, courage, confidence in God, peacefulness, a sense of safety around her – she is safe.

A letter

Dear St Melangell

I feel like that hare sometimes, running in a panic as though everything and everyone is set against me, and I know how precious it is to find refuge. I just love the idea of your mantle spread out as a safe space, a place to run to. Your protection is not in fighting but in prayerfulness – it's so lovely. All I want is to spend some time with you. I want you to put your cloak around me too, until I feel safe. Then maybe I can step back out into life feeling braver, but for now I just want the space to be held safely in compassion and prayer. I can't imagine you saying no, so I am coming anyway, but thank you in advance.

Yours in need of sanctuary,
a child of God

Aidan, died 651 AD

Aidan lived as a monk on Iona, coming originally from Ireland, and then was sent on to Northumbria to be the first bishop there, at the request of King Oswald who had grown up in exile on Iona. Aidan was the second bishop to be sent – the first had not been successful as he had found the local people difficult. The people in this region were not 'Celtic' but Anglo Saxon, largely descended from warriors and their families who had come over from Germanic lands as mercenaries after the Romans left, and settled.

In a 'supervision' meeting with the frustrated bishop, Aidan suggested taking a gentler approach, and he got the job. On arrival he chose the island of Lindisfarne as his base.

It became a significant site of Christian presence and has a reputation for 'thinness' to this day. At first, Aidan did not speak the local language and King Oswald went about with him as his translator. They became friends, but Aidan was equally willing and able to befriend the poor, cutting a figure not unlike St Francis of Assisi centuries later. He had a great regard for the poor, on one occasion challenging the king to feed from his own table the hungry who had gathered at the castle gates on the occasion of a feast – which he did.

Aidan preferred to walk everywhere – he gave away a horse – and when given money he would pass it on to those in need or save it to buy the freedom of slaves. Some of these freed slaves he brought to his monastery school, to be educated in the faith. His method of spreading the faith was to take time to speak to people at their own level, giving them 'spiritual milk' until they were ready to hear deeper truths. Aidan worked tirelessly to bring Christianity to the people. One of his students was Hilda, who established a monastery just down the coast, at Whitby.

Aidan lived during a time of unrest. King Oswald died in battle and was succeeded by Oswin, who also supported Aidan. Then King Oswin, too, was killed, and Aidan died very soon after, some say of sadness for the loss of his friend.

Qualities

Gentleness, patience, humility, integrity, willingness to serve, energy, compassion.

A letter

Dear St Aidan
You must be one of the gentlest, wisest, humblest people
I have heard of and I really wish to walk with you a

while, because I feel as though I have got lost in my faith. It has become all about me, all about believing this or that, whereas there's so much more to following Christ. If I could spend some time with you, I think it would help me to relearn what living the gospel is. I know I need to get back to the real practice of simple living and works of loving service; it doesn't even matter if I don't speak the same language as the people I want to help! I could do with your guidance on where to start – there's so much need in today's world, it's staggering. I think I've got 'compassion fatigue' – giving and giving exhausted me, and I let it beat me. Please walk with me a while and help me relearn how to give gladly and from the heart.

Yours in all humility,

a follower in need of redirection

Hilda, 614–680 AD

Hilda was baptised along with her royal Northumbrian household while still a girl, by Paulinus who had travelled with Augustine and followed the Roman tradition. She became a student and friend of Aidan, learning the tradition of Iona, and was appointed by Aidan to be abbess of the new Whitby abbey. This was a community for men and women who lived separately but joined for worship, and a renowned seat of education. A number of notable characters trained here from childhood.

In her own life, spanning from baptism to her position of leadership, she embodied the relationship between the two approaches to Christianity which were present at that time – the Celtic tradition linked with Ireland and Iona and further afield with the Desert Fathers and Mothers of the Eastern Mediterranean, and the Western tradition extending from the papacy in Rome. Both traditions were practised at that time, but they came into conflict, especially over dates for Easter.

Hilda was highly educated, an excellent manager and a wise counsellor. She was called 'Mother' by many. The abbey developed such a good reputation it was chosen as the venue for the Synod of Whitby in 664 AD – the meeting to resolve the tension between these two approaches. King Oswiu decided that Christian practice in the British Isles must conform to the Church of Rome because – so we are told – St Peter holds the keys to the gates of heaven, and Rome was seen as the seat of Peter's authority. This was a source of great sorrow to many as it spelled the suppression of indigenous 'Celtic' traditions, although they continued for much longer in Ireland. Hilda abided by the decision, with diplomacy.

Many, even kings, came to Hilda for advice, and she remained a friend of Aidan. She also had time for ordinary people, most famously a local cowherd named Caedmon, who had a natural gift for poetry. Through her support, he became known as the greatest poet in the land.

There is a legend that she turned the snakes in the area to stone, an old explanation for the presence of ammonite fossils on the beach at Whitby.

Qualities

Leadership, intelligence, valuing education, influencing others, recognising qualities and potential in others and being able to support and nurture this, able to find balance between points of tension, diplomacy, measuredness, balance, reason, a host.

A letter

Dear St Hilda

Since I heard about you, I have become more keen to explore my potential, what my gifts and strengths are that I can share with others. The work I've done in the past never really felt very satisfying or challenging, and I'm wondering how I can change to bring out more of the gifts God has given me, for the good of others. I think I've hidden away, and not been sharing as much as I could have done. I'd be grateful if you could spare some time to talk with me about how to live my life fully to the glory of God.

Yours in anticipation,

a willing student

Cuthbert, 634–687 AD

Cuthbert is said to have been a youth out in the fields watching sheep, and saw glorious angelic light from the direction of Lindisfarne the night Aidan died. This is what inspired him to pursue the holy life himself, although he seems to have grown up further inland. It was a complex environment where Christian and pagan kingdoms were in conflict, but so too were different approaches to Christianity. Cuthbert was trained in the Celtic tradition that originated in Iona, with the daughter church at Lindisfarne, but had frequent contact with followers of the Roman tradition that also operated in the region. One of the most vocal and active of the time was Wilfred, who is described as rather lacking in humility and with a penchant for big stone buildings and fine vestments.

Although the tradition of Lindisfarne and Iona was dear to him, Cuthbert submitted to the decision at the Synod of Whitby to step into line with Rome, and continued his ministry quietly from Lindisfarne, travelling widely. His preference was for a hermitic life, moving out from Lindisfarne to a small island, and then further out to the Inner Farne Islands to live alone with the seabirds and seals. This was in keeping with the Celtic tradition, inherited from the Desert Fathers and Mothers, of seeking lonely places in which to practise austerity and prayer. There are stories of Cuthbert's asceticism and prayer, and also his affinity with animals. On one occasion while at Lindisfarne, for example, he was followed by a younger member of the community who saw him spend the night in prayer, up to his waist in sea water, then come up onto the beach to be warmed by otters.

He was called to leave his hermitage to take a role as bishop, which he did with all humility, but before his death he returned to the island to end his days in peace. He became one of the most well known of the northern saints, and his coffin is at Durham cathedral to this day, inscribed with Anglo Saxon runes.

Qualities

Humility, asceticism, contemplative hermit, sense of commitment, solitude, love of nature.

A letter

Dear St Cuthbert
I really warmed to the story of your life, especially the way
you went to live on your own on an island and were then
asked to leave to be a bishop again. Some days, there's

nothing I'd like more than to go and live alone with nature, in peace. Maybe I am idealising – I'm sure it's not an easy thing to do. But the peace . . . Perhaps I'm feeling like that because I am in a role that I feel I've been pressurised into, and I'm doing it out of a sense of duty not because I want to. That weighs heavily on me, to the degree that maybe I feel like a bit of a martyr sometimes.

You might say 'No', because hermitages are about solitude, but I'd love to come and visit your island, to step into that peace, if only to take the memory away with me. I want a peace island in my heart that I can retreat to in my quiet times. I'd love to just sit quietly with you for a while in my peace place and watch the birds and feel understood.
Yours,
a frustrated contemplative

Ia, fifth or sixth century AD

St Ia grew up as a Christian daughter of an Irish chieftain in the mid fifth century. While still young, she learned of a missionary expedition over the sea to Cornwall and hurried to join it. When she got to the coast she found the others had gone without her, maybe because she was too young, maybe because she was a woman. Disappointed, she sat on the beach and cried, feeling abandoned and disappointed, and there she prayed. She prodded a small leaf that was floating on the water, with her staff, thinking it would sink. But the leaf, according to legend, grew and grew until it was large and sturdy enough to carry her. Seeing that God had provided her with a boat after all, she climbed in and the sea took her to the Cornish coast ahead of the others.

If this story seems too fanciful to engage with, we might see an embellishment of the story of a young person who overcomes self-pity through prayer and finds spiritual support in getting on with her life regardless of others. Setting off alone over the sea in a coracle (or a larger curragh), which was the normal way of getting about, is remarkable enough to us when we think about the fragility of the craft and the power of the sea. The leaf perhaps illustrates the sense of God's provision for her and God's affirmation of her desire to travel.

Ia survived the long and dangerous journey from Ireland to the north coast of Cornwall, alone in a leather boat the size of a modest dinner table. She then joined with other missionaries who had made a similar journey, and built an oratory – a little hut for prayer – in a woodland clearing near a sacred spring in the vicinity of what is now St Ives, attracting others to join the faith. Ia became influential in the area and as far away as Brittany, where she also has a church dedicated to her. Unfortunately she attracted the attention of a local king who did not like Irish missionaries and who, it is said, had her killed. The original church at St Ives was built over her grave.

Qualities

Courage, determination, prayer, openness to God's help, saying 'yes' to life's adventure, faithfulness, facing danger.

A letter

Dear Ia

The thought of you setting out in a coracle – or on a leaf? – over the Irish sea as just a young girl makes the hairs rise up on the back of my neck. I am full of fears

for my children, and there is no way I would want any of mine doing anything so dangerous. Yet you were fine. Your adventure led you to wonderful opportunities. People loved you – until you were killed, that is. See, my fears are justified – it's a dangerous world. But how rich your life was, and how deeply you were held in God's love. What do I know about any of our paths to death or the point of our lives? Not going, your life would have been diminished. You can see I am struggling with issues of letting go, and trust, and living life to the full but fearing accidents and attackers . . . I have a feeling you could help me calm down and trust life better, trust God. I'd like to learn about trust from you, if you could spare me some time.
Yours anxiously,
a loving parent

Govan, died 586 AD

Govan's tiny chapel is built in the crevice of a cove in Pembrokeshire, South Wales. There used to be two natural springs here which pilgrims would visit, but they have now dried up. The current building dates to the thirteenth or fourteenth century, but there was a place of prayer at the site long before. This marked the crevice in the rock where Govan used to live.

Legend has it that Govan came originally from Ireland, where his father may have been a blacksmith. It seems he joined a monastery in Wexford, Ireland, as a young man, attracted by the teaching of another saint, Ailbe, who came from Pembrokeshire. His monastery work may have been as a cook.

In time, and possibly after a journey to Rome on a liturgical mission, Govan travelled to Pembrokeshire himself, perhaps on the recommendation of his old Abbot and friend, Ailbe. Here, along the coast, he was attacked by pirates and escaped by hiding in a fissure in the rock that opened up just wide enough for him to squeeze in. (Visitors might still make out the marks where his ribcage pressed into the rock.) In gratitude for this miracle, Govan decided to stay at the place, offering up prayers of thanks, surviving on fish and fresh water from the springs and keeping a lookout over the sea, warning sailors away from the rocks and local villagers of the risk of hostile-looking landing parties.

It is said that he had a bell with a beautiful sound, which he used to communicate with the locals. It was stolen – by more troublesome pirates – and Govan prayed for it to be brought back. Angels obligingly brought the bell and encased it within one of the rocks of the cliff. When Govan struck the rock, it resonated with a clearer and truer sound than the bell itself.

Qualities

Dedication to service, witness to God's protection, gratitude, facing fears, vigilance and watchfulness, warnings of danger.

A letter

Dear St Govan

I love the idea of someone taking the trouble to watch out for danger – that is such a selfless and brave thing to do. Maybe it's selfish of me to want to stay with you just so I can experience that feeling of safety, but it feels really important. I live with a feeling of being vulnerable, and I don't really see much evidence of

*God's protective love in the world. With so much
suffering happening, even to prayerful, innocent people,
I don't see what right I have to ask for protection – yet
still it is something I want to ask for. This is something
I'd value thinking through with you: feeling safe, even
in risky situations. What does it mean, being safe and
being saved, anyway?*
With thanks,
a questioning soul

Madrun (or Materiana) late fifth/early sixth century AD

While Madrun's life seemed full of adventure, it is possible
that legends about more than one character have melded
together, as with Brigid. Madrun's name is also that of
a goddess of the Romano-Celtic era: *Matrona* in Latin – a
respected mother figure.

Madrun is mentioned as the only daughter of a Christian
Welsh king, son of the king Vortigern who was infamous for
inviting the Saxons into the British Isles after the Romans
left. Vortigern was not popular among his people. His son
inherited a fraction of the former kingdom, a small part of
northern Wales, where Vortigern had retreated after suffering
political disaster. Madrun inherited the little kingdom, in the
region of the Llyn Peninsula, and ruled with her husband.

At some point she made a pilgrimage to Bardsey Island, a
hallowed 'thin' place at the tip of the Llyn Peninsula, with
her maid Anna (another ancient 'mother goddess' name). A
Celtic Christian community was there, and Madrun and
Anna both received visions of building a church. (Although
it is a relatively short journey, it is no mean feat to go to and
return from Bardsey Island – the currents can be treacherous.

It used to be said that three pilgrimages to Bardsey Island were equivalent to a pilgrimage to Jerusalem.)

Madrun had three children while living as queen of an Iron Age hill fort and surrounding area, and enjoyed a period of peace while the older two grew up. Unfortunately, while her third child was still a baby, the hill fort came under attack. Her husband the king died in its defence, and she escaped with her infant son, taking refuge further south.

In time, her son Ceido became a monk and established a Christian community in the area. At some point following her flight from the fortress, she travelled to Cornwall. There she became respected not as an ex-queen but as a widow in holy orders. Madrun established churches which still bear her name to this day (the Anglicised variant Materiana), at Tintagel and Minster near Boscastle, where her tomb remained until the Reformation. Madrun is often associated with a crown.

Qualities

A 'woman of substance', willing to put past status aside and work for ordinary people, able to shoulder single parenthood following disaster and to secure a future for her son, confident, courageous, strong and self-assured, an archetypal 'mature mother' figure.

A letter

Dear St Madrun
I find myself strangely moved by reading of your life. I was especially struck by the way you did not need to tell people in Cornwall that you were an ex-queen, to win respect. I often find myself asserting my status in

different ways, subtly or directly – my identity is very much caught up with who I am in the world. Maybe it's a secret insecurity. I'm also struck by the way you made yourself available for public service with ordinary people, reaching out to them in the gospel. I don't reach out all that easily. If I am honest, I have a fairly low opinion of most people. That doesn't sound very Christian, I know, and I would not say it to most people, but I feel I can find some kind of rapport with you; you were such a strong character. I suppose what I'm saying is that I think you could help me find some humility, and also a confidence rooted in something deeper – Christ, rather than myself. I'm hoping we will be able to connect somehow.

With gratitude,

a respectful admirer

Brendan, 486–575 AD

Brendan was a monk and abbot in Ireland and is famous for a sea voyage which he and 12 or more companions made in a leather boat. They might have sailed all the way to America, and it certainly seems that there were communities of monks established on a number of remote islands of the northern Atlantic who hosted the voyagers at different stages of the journey. The accounts describe how Brendan's crew adopted a circuit of different holy sites on islands reachable by boat for a period of seven years, to spend Christmas, Easter and Pentecost in these isolated monastic communities. They spent the rest of the time out at sea, often fasting for long periods.

This pattern in itself might allegorise something of the Christian liturgical year, with its holy days and times of journeying through the hardships of life. After some years and many strange adventures, including experiences that sound very much like encounters with icebergs and volcanic eruptions, not to mention the close proximity of whales, a trusted guide on one of the islands finally said that he would show Brendan how to get to the land of 'paradise', which lay far away beyond a veil of mist. This they visited, and came home with many wonderful tales to tell. Brendan died soon after.

This journey expresses the courage and enormous faith of believers, trusting their lives to God by setting out in such a frail craft over such a mighty ocean. That people had the skill and confidence to make even small journeys between islands is impressive, but they went much further than this, stretching boundaries not only distance and danger-wise, but faith-wise too.

Brendan is well known for having Ita as his spiritual director and foster mother – see below.

Qualities

Sense of adventure, trust, faith, courage, skill, knowledge of sailing, boat-making and navigating, a desire to experience the wonders of creation, self-discipline, willingness to be guided, patience.

A letter

Dear St Brendan
You have such a fearless sense of adventure! I read the
account of your voyage with excitement and felt the

pull of the sea, calling me to set off on adventures of my own. I may not go as far as you did, but I can see myself just daring to step out a little further, to be a little bolder, a bit hungrier to see new things and be tested and stretched by new experiences. I can see myself in that little boat, blown about and soaked by waves, but pulling through each time. It makes me dare to feel safe, even though things don't look very safe. I like to think of Jesus being in my boat with me, like on the lake of Galilee, but you would be a good companion, too. I'd love to have some sailing lessons from you and some advice about staying afloat, as I've had some difficult times and have capsized more than once in my life.
Yours in gratitude,
a would-be adventurer

Ita, sixth century

Ita, also known as Deirdre, from Ireland, is said to have been blessed with spiritual experiences from childhood. She had a reputation for being very loving, and for prayer and fasting, although she lived in a household that had not fully embraced Christianity. On one occasion she was asleep in a room in the family home, which looked from the outside as though it was on fire. This turned out not to be the case: Ita was experiencing the glory of the divine presence and, on waking, continued to shine visibly for some time.

On another occasion she dreamed that she was given three jewels by an angel, which she understood to represent three gifts of the Trinity, especially that she would continue to be gifted with visions and wisdom to understand them.

As so often was the case, a marriage was planned for her, which she was not willing to cooperate with, but in this instance her father had a dream telling him that she was meant to lead a religious life. Even though he himself was not a Christian, this convinced him to let her follow her own convictions. She left soon after and established a convent, where she was made welcome by locals who offered more land than she needed. Here she continued in a life of prayer and fasting, and received more visions, one of which may have been the answer to a prayer that she might experience nursing the infant Jesus, and another warning her against excessive fasting.

Ita established a school for young boys, as monasteries often did, and was known as the foster mother of many of the Irish saints, including St Brendan, who continued to consult her into adulthood. He asked her on one occasion what three things most please God. She replied, faith in God with purity of heart, simplicity of lifestyle with prayerfulness, and a spirit of generosity inspired by compassion. She also told him that God most dislikes an unsmiling face, bitterness and faith in material goods or money.

Ita was known for her wisdom and holiness, and her sense of divine presence. She taught her students that the saints who had gone before them were soul friends. In turn, she was a soul friend to many.

Qualities

Visionary, closeness to God, spiritual gifts, prayerfulness, self-discipline, wisdom, companionship, sense of purpose, service through guiding and teaching others.

A letter

Dear St Ita

I have been through a very difficult time financially. There have been very real worries, and it has affected our quality of living. You said that God doesn't like us to rely on material possessions or wealth, and that God doesn't like us to go round with a long face either, and I'd like to talk to you about that. It's really hard not to worry, sometimes, and it's really hard when there is just not enough to make ends meet. I know simplicity and poverty are seen as spiritual, but trying to live in the real, modern world, you do need to be able to pay your way or it all gets very difficult. I'd like to talk to you about how to see my situation differently, how to bring my faith into my economic situation, how to stop worrying so much, and also how to help myself. The dreams I have are full of anxieties. I'd like to talk to you about that, too, since you have a reputation for inspired dreams and visions.

Yours in need,

a troubled soul

Columbanus, 543–615 AD

Columbanus, or Columban, meaning 'dove', was from Ireland. While pregnant with him, his mother had a vision that her son was going to be brilliant, and he did indeed shine. He proved to be a great scholar, studying in a range of disciplines as well as Scripture. He explored his spiritual vocation in two different monasteries in Ireland, the second being Bangor Abbey, renowned as a seat of spiritual vigour and asceticism. Here, already middle aged, he received a commission to travel to Europe with 12 companions, and it is for this missionary work and the strict rule of life he developed for the monks in his care that he is best known.

Columbanus travelled widely in Europe, establishing centres of Celtic Christian practice and getting involved in current issues of the time. He found himself in disputes about the date of Easter, well ahead of the Synod of Whitby, because his monks followed the Celtic rather than the Roman system practised on the continent.

He was not afraid to challenge what he felt to be moral lapses among the rulers he encountered. Although he challenged and spoke his mind, he did so quite lovingly and with a desire to communicate his understanding of gospel values. Interestingly, despite his willingness to wade in at the level of kings and queens, and in spite of his energy for establishing Celtic communities, he also had a retiring side and found a cave for himself in a secluded woodland, to which he often retreated with only one companion.

Several of the more endearing stories about Columbanus involve this wilderness-loving side. He is said to have had encounters with many wild creatures, not unlike St Francis of Assisi centuries later. In particular, he is associated with bears: he used a bear's cave for prayer and shelter at one point, and at another he shared an orchard with a bear, each respecting the other's half. He is portrayed as being in harmony with nature, understanding the need for simplicity of human lifestyle in not taking more than we need and in adopting a gentle, accepting approach towards the animal world.

Qualities

Passion for kingdom values, energy, promotion of the gospel, loving challenge, confidence in Christ, gentleness towards nature, a desire for simplicity or austerity, self-discipline.

A letter

Dear St Columbanus

I thought you might be a good person to talk to, as I have been working on a rule of life lately. I felt the need for some structure in my spiritual practice, and a little self-discipline, although I don't suppose my idea of self-discipline quite matches yours. While your rule is far more strict than mine, I get a sense of kindness from you, and I can't help thinking you would help me work out my own rule according to what works in my own life. I also think you would challenge me, hopefully gently enough, to stay true to the principles I am trying to follow, and to work out my relationship to community. I think you would help me go more deeply into my faith. I am especially attracted to the idea of coming to visit you in a quiet cave for a while, if that would not be too much of an intrusion into your peace. With respect,

a pilgrim on the way

Samthann of Clonbroney, died around 740 AD

Samthann (pronounced more like Savhan) was a Christian Irish woman of noble birth. She ran away from her husband either on the wedding day itself or close to the time of the ceremony, and took refuge in a convent. Marriages were often arranged, and this may well have been a bid for freedom from a situation to which she had not consented. In time, she became the Abbess of Clonbroney where she gained much respect, and was connected with the Culdees or Céli Dé, a movement intent on reclaiming the ascetic and disciplined character of Celtic spirituality.

There are numerous stories from the 'lives' that were written about her which show her to have compassion and a sense of humour and to be uncannily aware of others' thoughts. One account describes how she hired workers to fell trees and put up a wooden building. The foreman was secretly concerned that his team had not been given sufficient food to sustain them, and imagined a quantity of bread and cheese. Samthann apparently intuited his wish and provided exactly what he had imagined, laughing that nobody should be disappointed in their hopes.

On another occasion, when she was clearly in her senior years, sailors were bringing supplies of wool to the monastery from Iona, when a storm blew up. A boy in the crew rather irreverently said, 'Let's throw the old granny's wool overboard!' The storm died down, they arrived safely, and Samthann greeted the child with the question, 'What was that you were saying about me on the way?' She then told him that if he were ever in danger again, as he had been in the storm, he should not be afraid to call on her because she would know, and her prayer would help.

Some of her wise words have been handed down to us, including her advice to someone planning to go on pilgrimage, whose motives, it seems, she did not wholly applaud. She said that there is no need to travel anywhere in search of God, because God is always with us. When asked for advice on the best position in which to pray, she said something like, 'Pray in every position, standing, sitting and lying down,' as if to say that we should pray in all the activities of our lives, or pray without ceasing. To a student who said they planned to give up study in order to devote more time to prayer, she said that study helps to train the mind and concentration is an asset to prayer.

Qualities

The ability to express wisdom succinctly, compassion, concern for the welfare of workers, intuition, humour, the value of freedom.

A letter

Dear St Samthann

It is with interest that I heard of your advice to a pilgrim, that they need not journey since God is close wherever we are. I have meditated on this a lot. I have not been able to travel a great deal due to circumstances, but I have watched others leave, and wished them well. They are like migrating birds and I am like the robin that is here all year. To me, there has been a value in learning to love and know the place where I am.

I sometimes find myself alone – people move on and I stay here. There is a sadness in this. It seems to me that you have a lovely sense of humour, and perhaps you might help me to find some new joy in the silent solitude that I often live with. I would love to be able to communicate with you, if I may, and draw some support from your wisdom.

In peace,

a hopeful friend

Journaling

- In general, how did you respond to the saints?

- Who did you connect with most strongly and why?

- What correlation did you find, if any, between your preferred saints and your response to the Celtic cross in chapter 1 concerning your own inclinations, and your choice of archetype in chapter 3?

Journaling examples

I felt really drawn to the way Cuthbert just wanted to live in peace on an island. I went out on a boat trip to the Farne islands a long time ago and was staggered by the wildlife – all those birds. So I felt that I'd been to his home. But more than that, I could really relate to how he must have felt when they came to get him and told him he had to come back to the mainland to be a bishop. I bet his heart sank, but he went anyway and did his job. I feel like that about my work at the moment – I don't want to do it, but I can see why I need to just get on with it for now. It's helped me stop being so resentful about it.

I have this great image of sitting up near a cliff top looking out to sea, with the birds flying all around and Cuthbert sitting next to me. He doesn't say much but he seems very kindly and wise, a little rueful perhaps. I decided to link seagulls with Cuthbert – there are lots where I work; they scavenge rubbish in the park. When I see them or hear them now, I think of Cuthbert and I feel as though I have a friend who understands me.

Or

I wasn't sure about this exercise. I've never been that into saints. To me, Jesus is enough and I wouldn't pray to a saint so I wasn't really engaging. Then I came to Hilda, and she stood out. She seemed very modern – a high-powered and highly educated woman running a very reputable establishment, hosting a council that was going to change history. That stopped me in my tracks; she is someone I would really want to have beside me as I'm trying to make something of my life.

The other thing that struck me was her diplomacy: although the decision didn't go the way she probably wanted, she worked with that and kept her dignity – it wasn't the end of the world. I could learn from that. If things don't go my way I tend to overreact.

I've been searching for more on Hilda to get to know her better. I'd like to visit Whitby in the summer. The traditional symbol of ammonites doesn't really work for me – I connect her with my laptop. I've got an icon of her for my desktop wallpaper. If she lived now she'd definitely have one – she'd be organising and researching and communicating all the time.

Or

Over the winter, I had a challenging few months in which storms kept coming up both literally, in bouts of terrible weather affecting many, and psychologically, in my own inner world. I felt as though life was blowing me off direction and frightening me – there were so many challenging things I could not control. But while tidying a pile of books away one day (it's that kind of house, where piles of books can sit for a long time!), I came to Tim Severin's account, *The Brendan Voyage*, in which he describes his epic journey over the Atlantic with three companions, doing as the title suggests, retracing the voyage of St Brendan in a painstakingly made leather boat.

Brendan suddenly struck me as just the friend I'd like to have in a storm, with his complete trust in God and his strength and immense sense of adventure, but also his thirst for new experiences that would teach him more about the wonders of creation. Reading the book and reflecting on Brendan's courage in setting out over such dangerous waters in such a small boat, I found my bewilderment at current circumstances giving way as the faltering glimmer of a sense of adventure dawned. It seemed at the time that by finding the book, I was spiritually helped towards a more constructive and confident outlook because I opened my heart to the story of a hero of old.

Closing prayer

May the whole company of heaven
be coming and going through my door:
Brigid in her kindliness, daring me to share,
Aidan in his gentleness, showing me those in need,
Cuthbert of peace and love of solitude, calling me away,
and Samthann in her wisdom, bringing me back to find God
in the everyday,
here where I am,
and among my own dear ones.
Amen

Chapter 8
Connecting with creation

For every wild animal of the forest is mine,
the cattle on a thousand hills.
I know all the birds of the air,
and all that moves in the field is mine.

Psalm 50:10-11

Humans are not the only living beings we encounter in our journey. We are surrounded by creatures and plants, from the microscopic to the gigantic, and they belong in the habitats we so often control. We even host tiny life forms in and on our bodies, invisible to the naked eye but essential to our health. It may seem trivial to reflect on the presence of bacteria in our gut, digesting our food, or a bee as a companion living being, but if there were no bees to pollinate the flowers of the food crops we depend on, the survival of humanity itself would be in question. Remembering our connection to the earth is vital.

In terms of the Celtic cross, we can think of creation in relation to the circle spreading out in ever wider circles, the immediacy of the environment, the cyclical nature of so much of life and death. We can also think of creation in terms of the cross. The vertical beam expresses God's constant, living presence, now and always, the spiritual connection between 'heaven and earth' that asks us to view all creation as good and of God. The horizontal beam expresses the developments that have taken place on earth and in the wider universe since time began, and the future our planet is heading towards, whatever we consider that to be. We can draw spiritual and/or creative inspiration and wisdom from our own connection to the earth, which can add sublime beauty and great depth to our experience of life.

It might be of interest at this point to look back on your notes at the start of the book concerning your perspective on the Celtic cross reflection in chapter 1.

One of the most striking aspects of Celtic tradition is the incredible artwork of interlacing lines and figures, known as 'knotwork', in which a whole design is created from one single line; multiple intricate details are woven together. The impression is of interconnectedness as birds, dragons, dogs, leaves and tendrils all interweave with mystical spirals and labyrinths, knitted together into the fabric of these incredible creations. They suggest the interconnection of all creation, the finite entwined with the infinite, nature with the divine, and the Celtic cross becomes like a supporting trellis in a garden.

In this section we are going to reflect on some of the creatures represented in knotwork. Our human identity is bound up with all life, and we look to the natural world to learn more about ourselves. The first point of relationship is our food. Then we have some animals that work for us and some that live as our companions. We have plants that we enjoy tending because they are beautiful, plants that are the origin of our medicines, and plants that become our furniture and the timbers of our homes. Beyond the immediacy of our everyday lives, we may also enjoy garden birds, ducks on the pond, trees in the park, rainforests and their wildlife on the TV. We depend on fossil fuels, which are decomposed animal and vegetable matter from primeval forests; chalk is compressed sea shells from primeval oceans; rubber is the sap of trees . . . Our increased knowledge of the world through scientific discovery has revealed more than we can ever fully appreciate about the complexity of interrelationship. Then, of course, the animals and plants around us offer endless inspiration for creativity and, if we are so inclined, praise of the Creator.

Inspiration from nature and Scripture

One character who drew inspiration from the natural world around him, from the perspective of his own Christian faith, was Caedmon, a cowherd in Northumbria at the time Hilda was abbess of Whitby Abbey. He was very shy, and whenever folk held an evening's entertainment at which each made a contribution with a song or a story, he would creep off and hide in the cow byre. One night as he slept, he dreamed that a stranger came and stood beside him and said, 'Sing, Caedmon!'

He asked, 'What shall I sing?'

The stranger said, 'Sing of the beauty of creation.'

With that, Caedmon opened his mouth and a beautiful song flowed out. When he awoke he could still remember it, and his friends took him along to Abbess Hilda. With her affirmation he went on to become one of the greatest poets of the age.

Although there are ancient poems which may have been composed by Caedmon, such as the 'Dream of the Rood', we have only one fragment which is definitely attributed to him. This is found in the writings of the Venerable Bede (672–735 AD) – a monk, historian and natural scientist who lived in Jarrow, in Northumbria. Bede, like Caedmon, was Anglo Saxon, and by good fortune we have an Anglo Saxon version of the poem from which various people have made translations. For your interest, I offer two versions which I have translated myself.[5] The first tries to stay as close as possible to the Anglo Saxon word order and direct meaning (although the brilliance of the structure and poetry is inevitably lost in translation).[6] The second is inspired by the original but brings the language and thinking away from the Anglo Saxon penchant for heroic lords and noble fathers into the contemporary world of gender equality. In this second version I have moved the word order a little and taken a more 'free' approach, for the sake of the poetry itself. By all means focus on whichever you prefer, or look for other translations in other sources for comparison.

It seems likely that the following is only the beginning of a longer work – perhaps Caedmon's initial dream-song itself.

Caedmon's Song of Praise, version 1

Now we should praise the Protector of
the Kingdom of Heaven,
the power of the Creator and his perfect intention,
the work of the glorious Father as he established
the first of all created wonders: Eternal Lord!

He, the first Bard, for the children of earth,
set heaven as a roof: holy Creator!
Then, on middle-earth, mankind's Guardian,
the Eternal Lord, brought forth for them all,
the dry land: God Almighty!

---

5. Let me be the first to acknowledge the limitations of my Anglo Saxon. It is to me an enduring enthusiasm rather than an academic accomplishment.
6. I have worked from the Anglo Saxon text on page 206 of Bede's account of the Poet Caedmon, in *A Guide to Old English: Revised with Prose and Verse Texts and Glossary* by Bruce Mitchell and Fred C. Robinson (London: Guild Publishing, 1989 edition, first published 1964).

Caedmon's Song of Praise, version 2

Now we should praise the Protector of the heavenly realms;
the power and the wisdom of the One who defines
existence;the Source of all Glory's works, as the Eternal
Sovereign brought creation's primal wonder forth.

This One, the first to utter sound, the holy Creator,
made the skies to be a ceiling for the children of the earth,
then, for all peoples, drew forth the lands of middle-earth:
Guardian of Humanity;
Eternal Sovereign;
Almighty God.

In the spirit of Caedmon, you might find your own
thoughts drawn to Scripture – perhaps to the image of Eden,
or to Paul's words in the Epistle to the Romans, or perhaps to
the psalms. Below are some passages which might resonate in
different ways as you reflect on your own feelings about the
natural world.

Suggestions for reading

- Either skim over all the passages and, rather than trying
  to rationalise them, let one passage 'grab' you, then give
  time to reflecting more deeply on this, in whatever way
  suits you. Express your thoughts in your journal.

- Or visit each passage one at a time over several days – or
  even weeks. Read it slowly and meditatively rather than
  in an analytical way, until a line or a phrase 'speaks', then
  stay with that phrase for a while in contemplation. This
  is a 'word' or 'picture' for you to include in your journal.

From the second 'creation' account:

> Out of the ground the Lord God made to grow every tree that is pleasant to the sight and good for food, the tree of life also in the midst of the garden, and the tree of the knowledge of good and evil.
>
> A river flows out of Eden to water the garden, and from there it divides and becomes four branches. The name of the first is Pishon; it is the one that flows around the whole land of Havilah, where there is gold; and the gold of that land is good; bdellium and onyx stone are there. The name of the second river is Gihon; it is the one that flows around the whole land of Cush. The name of the third river is Tigris, which flows east of Assyria. And the fourth river is the Euphrates.
>
> *Genesis 2:9-14*

From the psalms:

> You cause the grass to grow for the cattle,
> and plants for people to use,
> to bring forth food from the earth,
> and wine to gladden the human heart,
> oil to make the face shine,
> and bread to strengthen the human heart.
> The trees of the Lord are watered abundantly,
> the cedars of Lebanon that he planted.
> In them the birds build their nests;
> the stork has its home in the fir trees.
> The high mountains are for the wild goats;

the rocks are a refuge for the coneys.
You have made the moon to mark the seasons;
the sun knows its time for setting.
You make darkness, and it is night,
when all the animals of the forest come
creeping out.
The young lions roar for their prey,
seeking their food from God.
When the sun rises, they withdraw
and lie down in their dens.
People go out to their work
and to their labour until the evening.

Psalm 104:14-23

From the prophets:

He said to me, 'Mortal, have you seen this?'

Then he led me back along the bank of the river. As I came back, I saw on the bank of the river a great many trees on one side and on the other. He said to me, 'This water flows towards the eastern region and goes down into the Arabah; and when it enters the sea, the sea of stagnant waters, the water will become fresh. Wherever the river goes, every living creature that swarms will live, and there will be very many fish, once these waters reach there. It will become fresh; and everything will live where the river goes. People will stand fishing beside the sea from En-gedi to En-eglaim; it will be a place for the spreading of nets; its fish will be of a great many kinds, like the fish of the Great Sea. But its swamps and marshes will not become fresh; they are to be left for salt. On the banks, on both sides of the river, there will grow all kinds of trees for food. Their leaves will not wither nor their fruit fail, but they will bear fresh fruit every month, because the water for them flows from the sanctuary. Their fruit will be for food, and their leaves for healing.'

Ezekiel 47:6-12

From the Epistles:

I consider that the sufferings of this present time are not worth comparing with the glory about to be revealed to us. For the creation waits with eager longing for the revealing of the children of God; for the creation was subjected to futility, not of its own will but by the will of the one who subjected it, in hope that the creation itself will be set free from its bondage to decay and will obtain the freedom of the glory of the children of God. We know that the whole creation has been groaning in labour pains until now; and not only the creation, but we ourselves, who have the first fruits of the Spirit, groan inwardly while we wait for adoption, the redemption of our bodies. For in hope we were saved. Now hope that is seen is not hope. For who hopes for what is seen? But if we hope for what we do not see, we wait for it with patience.

Romans 8:18-25

Response

We each respond to Scripture in our own way. As well as writing in your journal, you may wish to create something, however spontaneous or carefully planned. Caedmon did not plan to write a song and did not intend to become a great singer. Once we give our inner being a little freedom we can surprise ourselves – so listen to your dreams! Creativity, of course, takes myriad forms; maybe you are a community builder or a garden grower, a bike recycler or a child nurturer, even someone who loves creating order and simplicity where there was chaotic clutter. Identifying, valuing and enjoying our own expressions of creativity is part of our spiritual journey.

An extended journaling opportunity

Although numbered 1–4, the following activities could be done in a different order if this suits you better.

1. Imagine you are standing at the centre of the Celtic cross, with all creation circling around you. Draw concentric circles like ripples on a pond, with 'Me' written in the middle, as you have done for earlier exercises. This time, write down (or draw) the names of plants and animals in the circles spreading out from the centre, according to how 'close' they are to you. For example, a pet cat might be in the inner circle, the fish in the garden pond might be a bit further out, the heron that comes to try and eat the fish further out again.

   Return to the diagram to add things whenever you think of them.

2. Think about animals and plants on which you depend to sustain your lifestyle. How does the natural world meet your needs and wants, from food to furniture, clothing to work tools? Do some research, if necessary, to find out more about what some things are made of – if you use tyres on a bike or a car, for example, you are indebted to a rubber tree. You might find you also stray into the mineral kingdom – which, of course, is fine. There is no end to this exercise; it is something you can keep adding to as new things occur to you.

3. Further creativity: as with the creative response to Scripture above, you may like to write your own prayers or create something else in response to the theme of our interconnectedness with nature. Many people become a little like the reticent cowherd who thinks he has nothing to share. This may apply to you, in which case do take time to explore this. Creativity is one of the qualities that connects us with the Divine, and suppressed creativity is something like suppressed prayer. For some, creating something *is* a prayer. The voice that comes to you in your dreams might not say 'Sing!' but might say 'Build' or 'Grow' or 'Bake' or 'Birth' or 'Take photographs'!

4. To support your reflections, here are some prayers. Choose one (or more) that appeals to you and add it to your journal – or, of course, find one from a different source of inspiration.

All goodness you are to me, O God,
goodness of milk
and goodness of honey,
goodness of ripe grain growing
and goodness of bread,
goodness of broken bread and wine shared,
and goodness of hunger met,
your ever-flowing goodness
the blessing of your own self-giving love.
Amen

Christ in all
and Spirit in all,
O God of Threeness, filling all and spilling over
like the cup of rich blessings itself,
like the cup of rich blessings.
Nothing there is that is outside your presence,
nothing there ever was, nor will be,
that is outside the wide reach of your love.
Nothing, O Grace of all graces,
nothing is there in heaven or on earth
that is beyond your knowing,
unheard and unseen.
So, dear God, in the poverty of my own seeing,
and the poverty of my own hearing,
and the poverty of my own knowing,
let me find a footprint of your tread,
a feather of your great wings,
a reflection of your glory,
a breath of your presence
here and everywhere,
in my own heart and in all that I meet.
Amen

Oh the warp and the weft of the web that you weave,
and the perfect pattern of it all.
You like a spider spinning,
creating, adjusting, remaking, reworking,
you so patient, O Holy One,
you the sum of all that is;
the dead drawn back into you,
the new, bright and shining,
of your own self stretched out,
the whole, knit by gossamer threads of life itself,
the whole, knit by fine gold threads of yourself,
the whole, knit by threads of your own dear sacrifice of love.
Oh, the warp and the weft of the web you weave,
and the perfect pattern of it all.
Amen

Journaling examples

Here are some journal examples, from different voices, relating
to this section.

> I drew my concentric rings too small and quickly
> filled them up. Living on a farm (I don't work on the
> farm but some of my family do), I am surrounded by
> plants and creatures, so it was quite a challenge
> working out layers of relationship. I put the horses
> near the centre, Mungo closest of all. But each horse
> is different: they are like people; I have a different
> relationship with each of them. Then there's my
> greyhound Grendel: he's very close, but I'm not that
> connected with the working dogs. Same with the cats
> – they mostly come and go, a bit feral really. Mice are

way out! The cattle – I care about them as a herd but I don't feel attached like I do with the horses – they are more doing a job for us and we pay back by feeding and sheltering them. The farm grew up on the strength of the cattle, back in my dad's day, so we owe them a lot. We give them the best deal we can, but we also have to be economically viable so there's no room for sentimentality.

There's a big oak up on the hill that I go and lean against and watch what's going on, down among the buildings and around the fields. Often there's a buzzard or two circling overhead, or a red kite. I put the oak quite near the centre – it's like an old friend. Other trees have to be managed, like the cows, so there's not much room for sentimentality. They do hedging and some coppicing in the wood – it's about the whole environment rather than individual trees.

The wild animals I put further out. I know there are foxes and badgers around, stoats, shrews, hedgehogs, owls . . . and I suppose I know a lot about their habits. Like neighbours, we do our best to leave habitat areas for them, but I don't feel a great spiritual connection with them, especially the ones that are a nuisance. I think town people over-romanticise wild animals. They should see the carnage the fox makes if he gets in among the hens!

Or

I started asking what animals and plants I depend on, thinking it would be fairly straightforward, but even the list of food ingredients was incredibly long and I haven't finished. I got into more and more detail – honeybees, insects pollinating fruit flowers, worms in the soil, grain seeds, chickens and eggs – I don't eat meat but I eat eggs – and I wear wool from sheep.

I was looking around the kitchen – what about medicine tablets? I have no idea what is in these, but I know some plants give medicine. I might find out more about this. What about the appliances? They are metal – I guess that is mined and smelted; and the wooden table – pine, like the drawers. I cook and heat the house with gas, so that's decomposed vegetable matter – fossil fuel. I want to understand this better too, why exactly is it that burning fossil fuels is bad for the environment when burning logs is less bad (or am I wrong about that?)? On that note, I suppose I'm dependent on the forests to make the air breathable, too. Anyway, the list goes on and on and I haven't got out of the kitchen yet!

Or

Talking of creativity, when I was a kid I used to like drawing cars and planes but my art teacher told me I needed to diversify. I didn't want to diversify: I loved copying the different models, noticing how designers had found different solutions to specialisms like speed or manoeuvrability, and I could see they were thinking of animals – sharks, seagulls and so on. I could see the connection, but I didn't want to draw sharks and birds. Cars and planes are inspirational; they are inspired by nature. And the mechanisms are fascinating, too – the perfection of a machine working like clockwork, amazing precision and ingenuity. But I'm not supposed to like them; I get accused of not caring about the environment. Of course I care, but I still think these vehicles are works of art, and I want to understand the minds of the designers.

These days, of course, the emphasis is on creating green machines, and that's quite exciting. I'm really attracted to some of the aspects of green engineering, the problem of storing energy. If I were looking for an area to be creative in, I suppose it might be this.

Or

I put paints out for my grandchildren at the weekend and sat down with them for a change instead of leaving them to it. We made a real mess, but it was good fun. I let them show me how to mix colours, pretending I didn't know, and we finished up painting a big tree, using our hands to print the leaves. Celia had done it at school and she wanted to have another go. We stuck it up on the living room door, and it's been making me smile ever since.

Chapter 9
Creatures from knotwork

Praise the Lord from the earth,
you sea monsters and all deeps,
fire and hail, snow and frost,
stormy wind fulfilling his command!
Mountains and all hills,
fruit trees and all cedars!
Wild animals and all cattle,
creeping things and flying birds!

Psalm 148:7-10

Many of us feel an affinity with animals. Cats, dogs and horses often become beloved companions in life, so in this chapter we focus on the importance of creatures, expressed especially through art and mythology. Below are some of the creatures represented in Celtic knotwork by skilled craftworkers in Celtic and Anglo Saxon communities to illustrate the pages of Gospel manuscripts, some of which, such as *The Book of Kells* and *The Lindisfarne Gospels*, are still in existence.

We may encounter some of these creatures in our day-to-day lives, but we would be very lucky – or alarmed – to come across others. Most of these animals feature in Celtic legend and lore, which extends back in time to pre-Christian days (although most ancient legends of this kind were preserved for posterity by monks), as well as in the pages of illuminated manuscripts. Their pictures would have brought up all sorts of associations in the minds of those who drew them and first saw the artwork, all that time ago.

Read over the descriptions and, as with the human archetypes earlier, decide which creatures most attract or repel you. Extend the reflection if you wish by collecting pictures, folklore, legends, soundtracks, film clips and other information. You could even find opportunities to get closer, such as bird of prey handling sessions, to help you get to know more about the creature and its habitat. If you see this as more of a 'play' or 'inner child' activity for a bit of light relief, that is fine, but it is also fine to decide to go quite deeply in connecting with the animal that speaks to you imaginatively, creatively, spiritually and physically.[7]

If you find yourself drawn to a creature for negative reasons, ask yourself what it is that fascinates you, and what part of your life it speaks to. This is a book that explores opportunities for self-development and increased well-being, so rather than simply reinforcing identity issues – for example, a raven-like over-preoccupation with mortality – look for opportunities for positive change.

Preliminary spiritual accompaniment advice

In this section I describe more pre-Christian themes than elsewhere in the book, and while for most this will hopefully be of interest, for some it may offer an understandable challenge. Knowing our own boundaries – what feels safe and appropriate in our own journey and what feels 'off limits' to us – is part of respecting our own perspective – although we are always free to change our minds, and we need to allow ourselves the room to do this. Reflecting on the map of the Celtic cross, you might ask yourself where this section is taking you. Off road?

---

7. *Reclaiming the Sealskin*, 2002, *Wild Goose Chase*, 2006 and *The Healer's Tree*, 2011, all published by Wild Goose Publications, the publishing division of the Iona Community.

Beyond the circle? Deeper into the centre? You will, of course, be invited to journal about this at the end of the section.

Gaining background information can help us to form an educated opinion, just as familiarity with Scripture can give us confidence to explore, so let me offer three passages from Scripture that can be reassuring when venturing beyond our comfort zone. Please spend as long as you like reflecting on these before you proceed, or on others that seem more appropriate.

From the Epistles

So we have known and believe the love that God has for us. God is love, and those who abide in love abide in God, and God abides in them. Love has been perfected among us in this: that we may have boldness on the day of judgement, because as he is, so are we in this world. There is no fear in love, but perfect love casts out fear; for fear has to do with punishment, and whoever fears has not reached perfection in love. We love because he first loved us.

1 John 4:16-19

From the Prophets

Am I a God near by, says the Lord, and not a God far off? Who can hide in secret places so that I cannot see them? says the Lord. Do I not fill heaven and earth? says the Lord.

Jeremiah 23:23-24

From the Gospels

'See, I am sending you out like sheep into the midst of wolves; so be wise as serpents and innocent as doves.'

Matthew 10:16

The creatures

Deer

Deer were highly significant creatures in Celtic tradition, as they had been to people of Europe and Asia stretching back far into pre-history, when deer were part of the staple diet of early hunters. People's lives were bound up with the herds; they followed them and understood them intimately, and ultimately owed their own survival to the deer and other herbivore herds which roamed after the last Ice Age. The stag especially, with his branch-like antlers which could grow and bleed but which were cast off each year like the falling autumn leaves, was evocative of the trees themselves.

By Celtic times, some of the ancient ideas associated with human lives being physically and spiritually bound up with the deer had perhaps been developed into rituals meaningful to a farming community still respectful of but farther removed from the wild places beyond the settlements – as most of us are farther removed still. There are several stories from Celtic tradition in which hunters go on great chases through the forest to corner a stag with their dogs, only to discover that the stag is a messenger of the divine realm or the 'otherworld', and mystical experiences soon follow. In medieval Christian tradition, similar legends exist in which the hunter encounters Christ in or through the stag, who challenges the aggressor to become peaceful. There is also a symbolic association with Christ as a stag trampling on a serpent, evocative of the triumph of goodness.

Although hunting was still enjoyed, in practical terms, Celtic communities relied on farming rather than hunting for most of their food, and deer were a nuisance: they were difficult to keep away from crops because of their ability to leap high over hurdles and disappear into the thickets, silently as though invisible. This quality of apparent invisibility features in a story about St Aidan, who is said to have helped a fleeing stag by turning him invisible through prayer. In another, St Patrick and a companion became invisible to enemies by uttering a prayer, the 'Cry of the Deer', which turned them into deer. There is a term for changing from human to animal form or vice versa – 'shape-shifting', or 'skin-changing' – and there is a good deal of it in Celtic mythology, as though the human and animal realms were seen as close, perhaps interchangeable.

Stags are embodiments of the wildwood and of assertive, virile majesty. Does are their gentle consorts, beautiful and graceful. The deer is thus a creature with marked gender differences, illustrating what, in human terms, can become a stereotype of heroic male and harmless female. This can become a limiting way of seeing society and ourselves unless we find a way to see the two aspects of deer-nature not as the way 'real men' and 'real women' should be, but as complementary qualities within ourselves, both of which we need in order to be balanced individuals: nobility and gentleness flow together with the grace of deer.

Keywords and concepts

Hunter and hunted, self-giving, nobility, Christ, mystical experience, ancient wildwood, 'the old ways', virility and fertility, majesty, gracefulness, invisibility, shape-shifting, living beyond community, difficult to control, destructive (to crops and young trees), gender stereotype, balanced personality.

Eagle

Eagles are admired today for their majestic command of the skies, their ability to ascend high on thermals, and with their incredible vision, which makes them great watchers with penetrating sight and faultless, lethal aim, speed and power once they have selected their focus. Eagles were more common in days gone by than they are today; they were admired for their size and power, but not too welcome when lambs were about, for they could easily snatch up the farmers' prized young and carry them away.

Eagles were a key emblem of the Romans who occupied Celtic lands in the centuries just before and slightly overlapping the arrival of Christianity, and there may have been an ambivalent relationship for the people, with this symbol of foreign power. Myths from the Greco-Roman world circulated, in which the eagle is a bird of the gods, and of the sun. But there is also tradition that seems to reach back beyond the influence of the Romans, and a legend that the eagle is among the oldest and wisest of all the creatures on earth. When a hero on a quest sets out to find the lost youth Mabon, snatched from his mother as a child, he gets sent from one animal to the next, each older than the previous one, until he comes to an eagle. The eagle is by a small stone which he says was once a high mountain, back in the days of the eagle's youth, but there is one who is even older. This eagle directs him to the salmon, who knows where Mabon can be found. Through this chain of ancient creatures, the boy is found and set free from his imprisonment.

The eagle in illuminated manuscripts has a special significance for Christians because John the Evangelist is represented by an eagle, bearing the prayers of the faithful heavenwards. *The Book of Kells*, now kept at Trinity College, Dublin, has one of the most well-known and best-loved examples of such artwork. It is said that St Cuthbert was once journeying with a younger companion who was worried about how they would find food. Cuthbert pointed to an eagle and said God could provide food for them even by means of this eagle. Soon they came across her by the side of a river, with a fish in her talons. The youth went and took the fish as she dropped it, but Cuthbert criticised him for not leaving half for the eagle, who had done the work. So they left half of the fish for the bird and took the other half to enjoy a good supper with friends later on.

Keywords and concepts

Focused power, deity, sun, oak, renewal, light, prayer, divine provision, heights of heaven, transcendence, messenger or angel, perceptive, clear-seeing, above it all, fierce, aggressor or oppressing power, threatening presence.

Swan

Swans are much-loved inhabitants of our waterways and lakes today. The story children tend to grow up knowing about swans is that of the Ugly Duckling, by Hans Christian Anderson, in which a cygnet is brought up with a brood of ducklings. It struggles with identity confusion, discrimination and rejection until it finally discovers its true nature as something beautiful. This story was not known in Celtic times, but there are plenty of other swan stories that were.

Swans in Celtic legends often turn out to be innocent people under enchantment, especially beautiful maidens or children, and there is often a poignant love theme. In an Irish story of the young hero Oenghus, he dreams of a lovely woman whom he has never met and sets out on a long journey in search of her, eventually finding that she – Caer – is under enchantment and often lives as a swan on a lake with 50 or more other swans, her companions. He singles her out by a fine gold chain around her neck. Her change time is Samhain, a 'thin' time of year when strange things happen (in the Christian year this became the eve of All Saints' Day or All Hallows' Eve), and Oenghus watches and waits until then to become a swan too so that he can join her. Having transformed himself, he and the swan-maiden, Caer, fly off together. As they fly they sing or chant together, and their song causes everyone around to fall asleep for three days.

In another story, four children are turned into swans by an unloving stepmother. They have to live like this for 900 years, by which time Christianity has come to Ireland and a kindly saint, Kernoc, who lives beside their lake, takes care of them until the day the enchantment wears off. Sadly, as soon as they become human they do not resume their childhood but are very, very old and die, so Kernoc buries them with dignity and writes an ogham inscription (an ancient Irish form of writing) on their tombstone. In this legend (of which there are other versions), as in many others, we find intriguing overlap between the pre-Christian and the Christian world. Even though the old tales were perhaps 'Christianised', it was monks who wrote the stories down, which is a sign of how important the old tradition was to them. The stories still spoke to them, they recognised their value, and they gave them to us.

As with other water birds, swans were seen as particularly special in that they had access to three realms – water, sky and land – which gave them a status as spiritual beings, messengers of the 'otherworld' and difficult or unlucky to constrain. This and the migratory instinct meant that there was a strong association with spiritual freedom and of knowing more, having a bigger perspective on life than flightless humans. In more recent years the wild goose, which shares many characteristics with the swan, has been taken as a 'Celtic' symbol of the Holy Spirit, wild and strong, beautiful and free.

Keywords and concepts

Beauty, wronged innocence, purity, soul, patience, questing, enduring love, enchantment, being bound, finding freedom or being set free, sadness, living in 'in-between' states, not belonging, liminality, flight, the power of song and spirit.

Boar or pig

Boars occur a good deal in Celtic-style imagery and knotwork – for example, on grave goods of warriors unearthed by archaeologists, although they are hard to find in Christian illuminated manuscripts. They were seen as courageous, fearsome creatures which took a great deal of skill and bravery to hunt. Because of this they were naturally associated with warriors and with war.

Among the nobility – those who could afford horses – hunting was part of training for war, a young man's essential preparation for adulthood in a dangerous world. The association continued into medieval heraldry. Richard III had a white boar on his banner. This would have begun as an image of honourable courage but it is used in Shakespeare's play about the king as a source of insult, indicating a shift in attitudes towards pigs and boars from something noble to something ignoble. In Celtic legend it was considered a compliment to be named 'Pig', whereas today it is an insult; similar is also true of 'Dog', below.

Despite the boar's reputation for ferocity, St Kieran of Saigir in Ireland is said to have had a tame boar along with several other animals who lived like disciples with a teacher. The boar built a cell for the monk with his teeth or tusks – perhaps an allegory of Christ taming natural ferocity.

As with stags in many Irish and Welsh stories, cornered boars often turn out to be messengers from the 'otherworld', or people who have been changed into animal form. They are often not just animal objects to be slain and counted as trophies, or as meat products, but rather as meaningful, respected beings with a spiritual dimension.

Again, today, pig very much represents the objectified face of 'factory farming', the economical mass-producing of flesh, over and above regard for the nature of the living animal itself.

By the time Celtic Christianity was present, wild boar were not eaten as much as the domesticated pig, which was widely bred, being very popular with the Romans who encouraged pig farming until they left. Ownership of pig herds was thus an indicator of wealth. Sows were valued for their maternal qualities and high numbers of offspring, and boars for their virility. Pigs at this time were mainly let loose in woodlands rather than taking up arable land, where they foraged and helped to control the undergrowth as an integral part of woodland management. They would be let onto the fields before ploughing to help turn the soil over and manure it. So pigs were quite a helpful presence in the farming community, alive as well as being a welcome food source.

Keywords and concepts

Ferocity, courage, aggression, intelligence, virility, maternity, gender polarities or stereotypes, woodland management, nature exploited and objectified for economic motives.

Dog

At the time the illuminated Gospel manuscripts were created, dogs were highly valued for household and personal protection. Different breeds were essential for different kinds of hunting and for being brave, loyal and capable of obedient, controlled aggression. In legend, the prefix 'Cú' meant 'hound belonging to' and was used in the names of warriors. Young men would serve a warrior of a higher rank with fierce devotion and in return would receive significant gifts, signs of valour and honour. An army of such warriors was likened favourably to a prized pack of hunting dogs.

It seems dogs were often also associated with healing – probably because they lick their wounds. Pre-Christian statues in Europe have been found of gentle dogs associated with divinities at centres of healing, including statues of dogs as companions to women who may represent feminine aspects of the Divine. They were also felt to have a spiritual connection with the 'otherworld', as messengers and perhaps helpers, guardians or companions of those who were passing from this world to the next. In Christian tradition this role tends more to be under the remit of angels or of Christ, or of the prayers of the faithful. But how often does a sick or elderly person today draw comfort and companionship from a beloved pet dog or cat, a friend in the liminal place where life seems fragile, and death something that cannot be ignored?

There are many legends involving hounds, indicating how prevalent they were in Celtic culture. One such group of legends concern the hero Cú Chulain, often associated with dogs as though he embodies something of their qualities in human form. He obtained his name by inadvertently killing a warrior's guard dog and then vowing to take its place in service.

We tend to encounter dogs in the stories of the Celtic saints as packs of hunting dogs representing the aggressor, while we find ourselves empathising with the quarry – a hare, a boar or a deer. But they also appear as creatures to be pitied, such as the hungry dog which St Brigid fed with her father's dinner.

Keywords and concepts

Courage, loyalty, friendliness, obedient service, warrior, controlled aggression, hunting, pack behaviour, healing, intuition or connection to the spiritual realms, companionship including in suffering or dying.

Horse

Horses were much admired and valued in Celtic cultures, but they were – as they are today – quite high maintenance, so not everybody could afford to keep them. They were creatures that communicated something of their owner's status, not unlike cars today. St Aidan, like St Francis of Assisi some centuries later, is said to have been given a fine horse by his friend the king, for riding around the remote farmsteads, but Aidan gave it away to a beggar. His preference for walking and his making light of such a valuable creature were signs of his great humility – and his compassion for the beggar.

Horses were ridden, including into battle (although warriors often dismounted), and used for carrying loads and pulling chariots, but they tended not to pull heavier wagons and ploughs. Most harnesses for such work were made for oxen at this time, not horses. The speed at which people could travel on horseback made a great difference to communication and connection across the land: it opened up new horizons, brought news and new opportunities, and adventure as well as conflict.

Archaeological evidence implies that stallions and geldings were kept around the homesteads more often than mares, and therefore might have been broken in for riding and driving more often, while the mares may have been allowed to live together with their young, as free herd animals. The herding nature of horses is important but not always accentuated today. The way horses relate to one another, whether following a stallion or a lead female, was observed and worked with by the Celts, as with most ancient cultures that bred horses, including in the dynamics of military strategy.

As with does and stags (and sows and boars), mares and stallions represent strong gender differentiations which can become unhelpful, restrictive stereotypes when applied to human communities, but which can also give us insights into developing our own balanced personalities with elements of both: strong leadership and the power of the collective. In Romano–Celtic iconography, interestingly, the feminine Divine is often represented through equine imagery – most famously the deity Epona, adopted by many Romans.

Celtic riders trained from infancy, often choosing to ride bareback. They seemed to have an intuitive bond with their horses which meant they worked in harmony. One legend tells how the grey horse of a warrior wept because of its foreknowledge that the hero was going to die. A similar legend is told of St Columba: as he approached death, an elderly horse leaned close and wept in sadness. There is something of an intuitive bond, then, which many a rider today will attest to. This means that the value of horses is greater than their function or attribution of status. They are close, and they sense things which we cannot always sense; they are sensitive, with feelings and intelligence as well as courage and great stamina.

Keywords and concepts

Status, pride, value, battle, journey, news, speed, stamina, strength, courage, intelligence, leadership, the power of the collective, intuition, close bonds, communication and mutual understanding, affection.

Raven

Dogs, boar and horses represent a kind of heroic fighting spirit. They have qualities, perhaps, which indicate something of the emphasis in the 'Celtic' world on the need to be ready to fight, whether defensively or aggressively, and by women too, it has to be said, not just men (take Boudicca the warrior Queen of the Iceni as an example). But ravens help us to look at the violence of battle from a different perspective; they are often associated with ill-omen, the doom of impending carnage, the horror of bloodshed, cruelty and death. Ravens in legend also often have a feminine presence, an otherworldly knowing, and although this can be portrayed negatively, it reflects something of the worldwide female experience of war, as the archetypal sorrowing mother, wife, sister and daughter. Here we find the real emotional cost of aggression: the foreboding, the horror. Raven, then, from a Celtic perspective, is not a 'nice' image but a challenging one; it confronts us with a reality we might prefer to ignore.

There is a wider sense in which ravens are respected for their sharp intelligence. According to legend, the safety of the realm of England itself is bound up with the presence of ravens at the Tower of London. A great king, Bran, was slain unjustly in defence of his sister and, as he lay dying, he told his entourage to bury his head at the location which is now the Tower of London, where it would protect the island from invasion. Ravens, being Bran's birds, are encouraged or obliged to remain at the site, and we have ravens living at the Tower to this day.

The biblical association with ravens is much more positive, and we can turn to this, too, for our interpretation of ravens in knotwork. In the Bible, it is a raven that is first released from the ark after the flood. It is said to fly over the waters from then on, like the breath of God over the primordial waters in Genesis, until the time of a drought predicted by Elijah. Ravens then act as angel-like messengers of God to sustain Elijah in the desert.

In a similar spirit, St Cuthbert (there are a number of animal legends about Cuthbert) is said to have befriended a raven while living as a hermit on the Farne Islands. He scolded the bird for taking thatch from his hut, and the bird brought back lard for him to waterproof his guests' boots.

With the raven of Noah's story in mind, one great sea-voyager was Brendan. Although there are several theories about the meaning of the name Brendan, one is that it means 'little raven'. As someone so strongly inspired by God's Spirit to go out over the wildness of the sea, it would fit very well.

Keywords and concepts

Omen, having a 'bad feeling', fears of war, the pain of conflict, victims, loss, injury and grief, facing mortality, return to the earth, those who save us from danger, penance, protective presence.

Serpent

The serpents of Celtic tradition could include snakes, eels or even mythological dragons. The imagery and symbolism is quite mixed, even within Christianity. Snakes were seen to slide in and out of fissures in the earth and to shed their skins as though regenerating. Added to this, some were poisonous and to be avoided, or to be handled with great care – so there was an air of mystery, immortality, sexual insinuation and death wielding.

By the time a Christian presence arrived, the snake was also associated with the account in Genesis of the deception of Adam and Eve and their expulsion from the Garden of Eden, so a further association of deceit was added. In direct contrast to this, we find a number of serpents in the knotwork of the illuminated manuscripts which represent not satanic manipulation, but Christ. This is because of the way snakes shed their skins: they were thought to be 'reborn' in a sense, or to regain some vitality, and were thus a symbol of the resurrection body.

Some of the illustrations include splendid peacocks, which are not indigenous to the British Isles but might have been seen in small numbers by travellers and in the days of Roman villas. Peacocks, too, are a symbol of Christ. Interestingly, in other cultures, peacocks are paired with snakes because they are enemies. There may be a residue of this relationship filtering through into the artwork, but reinterpreted.

As with the dragon character Smaug in J. R. R. Tolkien's *The Hobbit*, in a number of old legends from northern Europe, large serpents guarded significant treasures. Others, or giant 'worms', lived down well shafts, causing a nuisance (even a terror) to local residents.

There were also deities of the old religions, male and female, depicted with snakes in their grasp or wound around their persons. To hold the snake is perhaps to imply that one holds its power; to hold the power of sexuality and death is to hold the power of life, too, as represented in the snake's sloughed skin.

Interestingly, there is some banishing of serpents by Celtic saints, most famously by St Patrick, who is said to have driven all the snakes from Ireland, but also by St Hilda of Whitby. There are natural ammonite fossil deposits on the beach near her abbey and people used to think these were petrified snakes.

Keywords and concepts

Sexuality, sensuality, regeneration, closeness to the earth, resurrection body, Christ, mortality, deception, venom, hoarding, the mistrusted and feared, the demonised, the mysterious.

Salmon

The salmon had great significance in Celtic legend. It was the oldest of all the creatures, able to reveal the location of the lost youth Mabon and thus help in his rescue and the achievement of a heroic quest (see Eagle above), and was especially considered to be the wisest of creatures.

A salmon was said to live in a pool or natural spring which was the source of the River Boyne in Ireland (although some versions give a slightly different location), surrounded by nine hazel trees which always had flowers and nuts on. These hazels were the true source of wisdom, and their nuts fell into the pool and were eaten by the salmon. Many sought to catch the salmon, to eat it and gain all wisdom and knowledge themselves, and one such was Fintan who fished for the salmon for seven years. Finally, he caught it and gave it to his apprentice to prepare, but the boy, Fionn, burned his thumb on the hot fat as the fish roasted over the fire. He stuck his thumb in his mouth to soothe it, and this was enough to give him the sought-after wisdom.

There are certain parallels between this and other stories of seeking a special quality, especially wisdom, which of course is an object of desire in the Bible too, at times personified as a beautiful woman (compare the quest for the swan maiden, above).

In Christian tradition, a fish has been a symbol of Christ from early times, the Greek word for fish, *ichthus* standing for 'Jesus Christ, Son of God, Saviour'. In the illuminated Gospels, such as *The Book of Kells*, a salmon-like fish sometimes appears close to a representation of Jesus, to make it easy to identify him. It is interesting to consider the connections that might have been going on in the minds of those who first saw the little salmon illustrations – it might have seemed that a strong identification was being made between Christ and wisdom, which indeed is an association made by the New Testament writers themselves.

Keywords and concepts

The ancient, the primeval, wisdom, hazel, natural spring, that which is sought, the power of bards, knowledge, poetry, water, feelings, inspiration.

Journaling: how do you feel?

Before you go any further, update your journal with as much explanation as you wish about your response to the animals, including your feelings about the whole section. It might be that it excited you, putting you in touch with a fascinating world of ancient legend that pre-dates and interweaves with Christianity, or it might be that it made you feel uncomfortable, for a similar reason. Write about it – and perhaps your response to the three Scripture passages too.

Go back to the keywords and concepts, and let three speak to you:

- a 'challenging' trait that you are aware of in yourself that you could work on

- a quality you feel you already have

- something you aspire to or admire in somebody else.

If there are qualities or traits that occurred to you but which are not listed, feel free to add them. If you enjoyed reflecting on these creatures, you might go on to think about the habitat your favourite creature lives (or lived) in and whether there is any connection with the inclination you chose in chapter 1.

Journaling example

Here is an example of an animal archetype journal entry:

> When it came to the animals, I wasn't sure what the point was to start with. I just picked dog because I like dogs and see lots of qualities in them. But then in church I noticed the eagle lectern. I saw it in a new way: a huge golden bird with outstretched wings soaring upwards – I'd love to see a real one. I could suddenly see how majestic it was. I liked the idea of it soaring higher and higher with its amazing eyes looking down and seeing every detail. I sensed the spirituality, the transcendence, the joy, and that's the joy I feel in Christ that I want to share with other people. But it's not flapping madly up there; the air is lifting it up – it's God's Spirit that lifts people up. I can't lift people up; I can just be me. So an eagle archetype seems to have spoken to me most.

Keywords and concepts

Challenging trait: I think I have some 'controlled aggression' in me, which is maybe the downside of that friendly dog I nearly chose. I can get a bit like a pack animal and start joining in with 'attacks' on others, even if it's nothing really to do with me.

A quality that I have is sensuality. I'm really in touch with my body and I see that as a healthy, good thing. I like people to find me attractive. I like being physically flexible – that's a word I thought of connected with snakes.

I aspire to being more joyful and I associate this with the eagle, although it isn't in the list.

Closing prayer

Wise salmon you are, for the seeking;
great eagle you are, of soaring prayer;
fine swan of love and true voice of raven,
the song of love and the cry of sorrow,
both are known to you.
New life of the shining snake is yours;
sacrifice of the noble stag is yours;
true knowing of our minds is yours,
like faithful horse, like kindly dog,
true companionship is yours and loving service,
and so it is for we who follow,
to learn your ways, O Christ of many blessings,
O Christ of many shapes and none.
Amen

Part 4

What time is it?

Chapter 10
Cycles and holy hours

You have made the moon to mark the seasons;
the sun knows its time for setting.
You make darkness, and it is night,
when all the animals of the forest come creeping out.
The young lions roar for their prey,
seeking their food from God.
When the sun rises, they withdraw
and lie down in their dens.
People go out to their work
and to their labour until the evening.

Psalm 104:19-23

In this section we explore a number of different ways in which the Celtic cross can help us locate ourselves in the passage of time. Time is measured by observation of the sun – hour by hour, season by season, year by year – and of the moon, month by month. This theme reconnects especially with the cyclical element of the Celtic cross reflection in chapter 1, which is depicted as a sun or moon in the sky. You may wish to go back to this point with fresh insight when you have read further, especially if you were not sure initially whether you wanted a moonlit scene or a sunlit scene in your inclination picture. Both sun and moon express the cyclical experience of life in fundamental ways – the moon in its orbit around the earth and the sun as the centre of our solar system, around which we travel in our yearly journey.

As an introductory activity, jot down answers to as many of the following questions as you wish, based on the present moment. Of course, you can research your answers. It might interest you to look back at your answers later on.

- What time is it now?

- What day of the week is it?

- What phase of the moon is it?

- What season of the year is it?

- Which of these solar events has most recently happened or is approaching next?

  winter solstice (around 21–22 December)
  spring equinox (around 20–21 March)
  summer solstice (around 21–22 June)
  autumn equinox (around 22–23 September)

- What season or holy day of the liturgical year is closest?

  Advent
  Christmas
  Epiphany
  Lent
  Easter–Pentecost
  All Saints and All Souls, the Annunciation,
  Candlemas . . .
  ordinary time
  a special Saint's day

- How would you describe your present life stage?

  youth/teenage
  young adult
  mature adult

elder/senior

very elderly

a different term ('maiden', 'mother' and 'old wise woman' or 'crone' are popular terms in some circles, or you might like to acknowledge a rite of passage, such as newly married, retired, parent of teenage children, and so on)

- If you have a set daily prayer time, when is it?

- If you have a favourite time of year, what is it?

- If you feel especially drawn to one of the Church's holy days or seasons, what is it?

Marking the passing of time

The circle of the Celtic cross is a little like the circle of a clock face, marked by the intersections of the cross at twelve, three, six and nine o'clock. We can locate ourselves in time by noting the position of the sun and its shadow, the shape of the moon and the seasonal changes, as people have been doing for a very long time. Archaeological remains around the world indicate that people were watching the heavens and constructing fascinating structures which charted the passage of time. It seems that they also celebrated it ritually – from a spiritual perspective – and used the special natural effects to create moments of wonder. It was with great interest, for example, that I remember reading, some quarter of a century ago, a suggestion in an old university library book that the first temple as described in the Bible was built with its doors facing east, so that the dawn light on a particular day would shine in and reflect off the gold panelling within: a light show of dazzling glory!

The Celtic Church recognised the importance of the natural calendar and wove its own liturgical days and years into the great cycle. The Church year gives us a way to locate ourselves meaningfully in the bigger picture of the earth's journey through space. This can be both a personal location, depending on our own feelings and circumstances, and a corporate one, sharing with others within the wider faith tradition. The circle in the Celtic cross can stand for this liturgical cycle, just as it can stand for the natural passage of time. By reflecting on such cycles, we can regain something of the sense of order and pattern to our days, as well as a sense of proportion as we realise our smallness in relation to the cosmic dance.

Surprisingly, perhaps, one of the Celtic saints most clearly identified with the importance of the Church cycle is St Brendan, who is most famous for making what sounds like a linear voyage from Ireland to America in a small boat. Although an important aspect of his voyage is that he and his companions did indeed find their way to the paradise-like land of his dreams by sailing west over the sea, the bulk of the account is taken up with the seven years prior to this discovery, in which he and his companions, all monks, made a circuit of islands, including it seems, the Hebrides and the Faroe Isles. They would spend Christmas with one remote monastic community, Lent and then Easter with another and Pentecost with another, while the 'ordinary' times they spent out on the wild seas, fasting and exposing themselves to all kinds of dangers and wonders.

This cycle of seven years in itself can be seen as an allegory of the stable continuity of the Christian seasons and the common experience of monastic prayer life, the chanting of psalms and offering of liturgy, and the open spaces of exposure to life itself, the stretches of sailing over the open sea, with all its challenges – in which time, of course, the brothers in their boat continue to chant the cycle of psalms and say their daily prayers. Brendan the voyager, then, is firmly held by the discipline of the Church calendar, and it is only after seven years have passed that he learns how to move on beyond the cycle to find what he is searching for. Seven years is a traditional period of waiting and preparation for something special – Jacob waiting to be able to marry Rachel, for example (Genesis 29:18-20) – with guidance from somebody with experience. We, too, belong in the natural cycle, and can find peace through attuning to it, yet all the time our hearts may also yearn for liberation from the same.

Below are some descriptions of the passage of time. Some of these are from the perspective of the natural cycles, some from the Celtic Church and some, of course, from the traditions of the wider Church. As you read the descriptions, you might at times want to refer back to earlier sections on direction and location, since there is a relationship between the measurement of time and direction.

As you look over the descriptors, think about what season it is at the time of reading, and what naturally follows. Think, too, about what times, seasons and cycles you especially notice and which resonate with the way you feel at the moment. There are journaling examples at the end of the descriptors.

Holy hours

If the Celtic cross is seen as a clock face, the arms of the cross mark out four special hours: twelve, three, six and nine, on which we will reflect below. The early Church practice of honouring set times of the day and night was directly influenced by Jewish worship patterns of morning and evening prayer and sacrifice which we can find detailed in the Bible, and also by the structure of Roman city life which was punctuated by bells striking at regular intervals to govern daily business. The empire's commerce, councils and labour revolved around these bells, which Christians made use of as a call to prayer and a reminder of allegiance to Jesus as Lord rather than the emperor, whether momentarily as they continued their work or through gathering with others in liturgy.

There is also an association between the hours and the accounts of Jesus' trial, execution and death. The Gospel writers tell us at which time particular events were thought to take place, and we can take these at face value or interpret them as the writers drawing the immediacy of Christ's death into the everyday by linking the Passion to times that were already notable in the structure of the day for readers and hearers living in a Romanised world, as most were by the time the Gospels were written, from 70 AD onwards. From a Jewish perspective, which of course was the culture in which Jesus and his disciples lived, the natural patterns of sunrise, noon and sunset were of equal or greater significance than the regulated 'hours', as the sun's setting dictated when one day closed and a new day began. Reading the Passion narratives, we find that as well as specific references to time, we find events located according to the first light appearing, a rooster crowing and evening approaching, marking the beginning of the Sabbath.

The tradition of praying with the hours developed quickly in the Church centred in Rome, and spread abroad to become established monastic practice, including in Celtic

Christian circles. Regional variations developed regarding times, emphasis and prayer routines. Today there are a variety of different practices we can engage with.

As you read through the following hours of the day, consider how they relate to your own routine. If you have a lifestyle that follows a very different pattern, perhaps because you work through the night, think about how the times can be meaningful in your own context: dawn might signal the end of your shift, for example, and the anticipation of rest, rather than the start of the day.

Twelve o'clock

There is an early Church tradition that says that at midnight, all creatures pause momentarily to praise God their creator. Christians too used to (and some still do) rise from their beds to join their praises to those of the rest of creation. Of course, midnight is a time of darkness, yet this darkness is periodically alleviated by the presence of the full moon at its highest point in the sky. This can be a time of mystery and wonder, of stillness and peace.

By midday, the sun is at its highest point in the sky and many are engrossed in work or looking forward to their lunch break. There may be work to bless, or food to give thanks for, children to look after, people to meet with, or simply the morning to review and the afternoon to contemplate, but this, again, is a moment to pause and to acknowledge or invoke the presence of God in daily life.

Although midday might normally be seen as a radiant, positive, affirming time of joy and energetic activity, a time for thanksgiving and gladness about life itself, on Good Friday, midday marks the beginning of three hours of sorrowful reflection. This is because, according to the synoptic Gospels (Matthew, Mark and Luke), between the 'sixth hour' and the 'ninth' on the day of Jesus' crucifixion, the sky went dark and remained so until Jesus died (Matthew 27:45, Mark 15:33, Luke 23:44). The sixth hour is normally understood in English translations as midday, and the ninth hour as 3pm. The hour at which Jesus is said to have been crucified in this narrative (Mark 15:25) is the third hour, or 9am (see below), so Jesus had already been on the cross three hours before the clouds rolled in. The synoptic accounts contrast with John 19:14, however, which states that 'about noon', or the sixth hour, Jesus was still with Pilate. (This is a whole day earlier than in the synoptic accounts: the day of preparation for the Passover, rather than the Passover itself.)

Three o'clock

In the human sleep cycle, the 'small hours' between 1am and 3am are when many of us are – or want to be – most deeply asleep. To wake and pray at this hour requires special effort, yet some, including people of other faiths, still do so. Even while most of us sleep, some around the world are praying, just as some are working. The watchful presence of God and the holy angels through the night is often referred to in prayers from the Celtic tradition: we can take our rest and sleep in peace knowing this time is holy whether we are awake or not. In the summer, in some parts of the world, 3am is close to the time of the dawn, a natural time to rise, pray and get to work. It can be a special time for people on nightshift or who are unable to sleep because of their troubles: they are not awake alone.

In terms of the Passion narratives, we might associate this time with the all-night meetings that are described as taking place in the Gospels, during which Jesus was interrogated by a council responsible for maintaining the Pax Romana during the Jewish festival, while Peter is said to have waited fearfully in the courtyard below. When and if night-time worries keep us from sleep, there is food for thought that may bring things into proportion, in the fate of the imprisoned, often enduring injustice and brutality in our world today.

Three o'clock in the afternoon is a different matter. By this time many of us are experiencing a natural lull in our body clock, an afternoon sleepiness with which we may have to contend in order to get on with the day. This is the time at which Jesus is said to have died (Mark 15:34 and other synoptic Gospels), and therefore calls for a moment of sombre reflection. In addition, in the winter in some parts of the world it soon begins to get dark from this point on. Our prayers at 3pm might be for a renewal of energy, for refreshment and for a sense of purpose.

Six o'clock

Although our experience of dawn depends on the time of year and where we are in the world, 6am is a good general 'early morning' time. At this time we may well be awake or we might still be wrapped up in the dreams we will wake up remembering most clearly.

For those who wish to greet the true dawn, it is easy to find sunrise times on calendars and on the internet, and again, we will not find ourselves praying alone, for people of many faiths pray just before, during or just after the dawn. Christianity finds symbolism inherent in the sunrise, as a call to remember Christ's resurrection. It can be seen, therefore, as the most joyous time of day, and a time to commit all that we do to God.

Later in the day, 6pm falls around the time many are concluding a day of work and heading home, anticipating or already enjoying the process of mealtime and perhaps the companionship of family or friends, or simply the opportunity to relax a little. In the 'real' world, however, it is not necessarily a restful time; the day is by no means over. By this time in the winter it is already dark; evening has begun: it is a natural time of closure to mark the setting of the sun.

As with sunrise, sunset is an ancient time of shared prayer. It is easy to find sunset times on the internet should you wish to honour the precise moment. In Jewish tradition, the evening marks the end of one day and the beginning of the next.

Nine o'clock

By 9am, the world of work is in full swing, and not in a position to stop for prayer or for anything else. Even if we ourselves are not busy, it is worth reflecting, with compassion, on the necessity to work and the implications of what we are required to do. Prayer might focus on everyday tasks in the household or the workplace – as in so many of the prayers from the Celtic tradition – seeking peace in our work or seeking to support others in their work.

In terms of the Passion narrative, Jesus was crucified at the 'third hour' (Mark 15:25), normally understood as 9am. For the Roman soldiers on that particular morning shift, 'work' involved executing Jesus and others. According to Luke 23:34, Jesus forgave them because they were acting in ignorance. What we do and why we do it, who we are working for and who profits or suffers from our labour are always things to bring to prayer and reflection.

Even under pressure, the very act of looking at the clock can be a reminder of the call to pray without ceasing, simply by our attitude, our manner, our words, our decisions and our actions as we engage with life, although this is something we might aspire to rather than achieve. Those who have the time and inclination to pause for prayer at this time, as always, find themselves part of a great network of prayer around the world, Christian and otherwise: morning prayer for many falls between 8am and 10am.

While all our lives are different, everyone needs times of relaxation and reflection, and by 9pm many are entering into that relaxation time in preparation for sleep. In the Church pattern of prayer, Compline – a gentle, candlelit night prayer – often falls around 9pm. This supports the natural process of letting go of the recent past and entrusting ourselves to God's care through the night. Many of the prayers in the Celtic tradition concern this pre-sleep time. Celtic night-time prayers are often to do with trusting in the care of God and the holy angels, especially St Michael and the ever-loving Mary. Prayers from an age where day-to-day life was far more precarious reveal how people did not take for granted that they would wake in the morning. The Archangel took on the role of 'psychopomp' – the one with care of souls in sleep but especially in the great journey of death.

The cycle of hours brings us back to twelve o'clock, whether joining the natural praise of all creatures for their creator at midnight or invoking blessing on our daily food, companions and activity at midday.

Journaling

There are many ways of practising a prayer life, from sitting in silence to just 'talking to God' whenever we feel the inclination; from using a repetitive prayer such as the rosary to working our way through a printed scheme or a traditional daily office, alone or with others; or finding a beautiful place outdoors where we feel at peace or re-energised. For some, it helps to have a pattern to prayer, or to share the same words as others – such as the 'Our Father'. For others, it does not!

- What are your thoughts on the tradition of praying at specific times of the day and night, and of connecting these times to natural cycles?

- What does prayer mean to you, and how, if at all, do you yourself pray or consciously relate to God?

A prayer

Christ at day's dawning,
Christ at day's fullness,
Christ at day's twilight
and Christ at day's close.
Christ in my heart
and Christ in my thoughts,
may Christ be the true sun of all my days.
Amen

Journaling example

I follow a pattern of prayer, getting up at 7am every day to say my daily office in my study. Even though I am alone, this gives me a great sense of connection to the wider Church, and to the Christian story as I think of my brothers and sisters around the world joining to do the same thing. Even though most of the words are the same day by day, it never ceases to amaze me how one word has great significance one day, and another day an entirely different word or passage speaks to me. I love the way the psalms vary, and look forward to finding out what the psalm for the day is going to be. It often turns out to be very relevant as the day unfolds.

This is a special time, and if I cannot do this for any reason I find myself out of sorts. I can appreciate the value of linking this to an appreciation of the time of day, of course, as I do this at the same time every day. In the winter it is still dark and the candle seems extra specially important, and for two periods in the year dawn is rising. Then, of course, in the summer, it is already daylight and the birds are singing away. I could do more to be aware of what is going on in the natural world around me as I pray; I could make sure the curtains are open so I am more aware of the light – even open the window maybe, to share with the hedge sparrows.

Or

I have a very busy life, which sometimes seems a bit chaotic. It is difficult to develop a routine; every day is different. It is also difficult to stop: right up until bedtime I am on my laptop or on the phone. I am very sociable and enjoy the buzz, but sometimes it all catches up with me and I go into hiding with my earphones and a good book. I do try to go on a weekend retreat every year or two. These often end up quite people orientated too, although I have done a silent day, which was a challenge: I didn't know what to do with myself after the first hour.

Prayer, for me, is on the hoof. I have an ongoing chatter to God: I ask for help with anything and everything, from the traditional request for a parking space to giving feedback to a colleague, to picking the right train tickets. I involve God in everything, and on a good day it all flows, it all seems to generate more energy. Praying at set times of the day – well, I'm not sure I need it, although I really like the associations with different times, especially the links to the life of Jesus, and the idea that even if I am working at night, there are people who are also awake and praying. I really love the idea that all the animals praise God at midnight – I feel quite inspired by that idea. I'm often awake at midnight. It made me think of the last line of the last psalm:

Let everything that breathes praise the Lord!
Praise the Lord!
(Psalm 150:6)

Chapter 11
Moon months

The moon is relatively easy to observe, especially for people who spend a lot of time outdoors. It is not as easy to make sense of the moon's behaviour, which is always changing. It appears at different times and in different places depending on its stage in the cycle, a cycle in which it seems to grow from nothing into a thin crescent, then a luminous orb, and then shrink away again to nothing. Like the sun, when it is visible the moon gradually moves across the sky, sometimes in daylight, sometimes at night. To people without the full benefit of astronomical information, it is no surprise that the moon is an object of mystery and power. The Bible acknowledges that this sense of mystery sometimes understandably expands into worship (Wisdom of Solomon 13:1-9), as with the sun, but asks followers of God to differentiate between the wonderful Creator and the wonders of creation.

Great minds through the ages have gradually worked out what is going on in the journey of the moon, sun and earth. The moon is in fact orbiting the earth each lunar month, which is, along with a host of other planets, in turn orbiting the sun in its yearly cycle. This suggestion shocked the religious authorities in the days of Galileo; they wished to maintain the assertion that the earth was the focus of attention, the centre of existence around which the heavenly bodies travelled.

I have found that in workshops, the moon's cycle tends to be the one people are less familiar with, so I will give a little background information at this point. Peoples all around the world and stretching far back into prehistory have used the moon to measure the passage of time by counting the days from one stage of the cycle until its repetition roughly 28 days later – a single orbit of the earth. There are almost 12½ repetitions of the lunar cycle within a solar year.

Judaism and Islam still follow the lunar calendar and, indeed, Christians do too, in calculating the date of Easter, which is associated with the Jewish festival of Passover and dependent on the moon's cycle. There are many references to phases of the moon and the celebration of lunar sabbaths in the Bible. It is curious, given these scriptural roots, that Christianity and the secular West has inherited a solar calendar from the ancient Greeks and Romans, the dominant power at the time Christianity was emerging as a separate faith.

There is a mismatch of about 11 days between the solar calendar and a count of 12 lunar cycles. Judaism makes an adjustment so that named months remain within their proper seasons – Nissan, in which Passover is celebrated, is always in the springtime. In Islam, the months are not adjusted and gradually move into different seasons so that, for example, if the holy month of Ramadan begins on 12 July one year, it will begin on approximately 1st July the year after, and then mid June the year after that.

The lunar months were also counted in cultures of the northern hemisphere, with some adjustment (the insertion of an extra thirteenth month every few years) to make sure the months fell at around the same season each year. They were named accordingly. According to Bede, for the pre-Christian Anglo Saxons, the moon month around May was the month of 'three milkings', when the cows were milked three times a day; August's moon-month was 'weed (or vegetation) month'!

It has often been said that the moon is sacred to or significant to women, because the lunar cycle is approximately the same length as the human menstrual cycle. This has been especially explored among women in contemporary forms of Judaism, and also in some forms of earth spirituality, developing interesting rites and reflections on the spiritual phases described by the moon.

The moon is strongly associated with water, and it was the eighth-century monk, the Venerable Bede again, who worked out the gravitational influence the moon has on the earth's oceans, causing the tides. Water is often seen as a symbol of our unconscious, and thus of our deepest feelings, dreams and impulses.

Returning to our reflection on the usefulness of the Celtic cross as a map, we find that it can represent a simple version of the cycle of the moon. The highest point of the cross marks the full moon; the lowest, the new moon. The two outstretched arms mark the halfway points – first, where the moon is waxing or increasing, and second, where the moon is waning or decreasing again. Travelling around the circle, we pass through the weeks, of roughly seven days each, from new moon to first quarter, then on to the full moon a fortnight later, and then another fortnight goes by as the moon gradually wanes back to darkness. The circle of the cross thus acts as a calendar of a whole lunar month.

Many have seen symbolic, often spiritual, value in the phases of the moon, and how they can help us reflect on our own experiences. In the following descriptions, we will focus especially on the moods or phases of our spiritual life.

New moon

The most distinctive stage is the appearance of the new crescent at sunset after a few days of darkness. At this stage, the moon is in the west. To get to this position, it has been travelling through the sky during the daytime, as it was during its dark moon phase, so we could not see it because the light of the sun is so much stronger. Watching for the appearance of the new crescent has occupied minds for a very, very long time, and its appearance is a traditional sign to gather together for a celebration or for ritual observance – a sabbath.

The new moon, then, represents renewal, gladness, a bright new beginning, an opportunity for re-dedication whether alone or in company. It is appropriate to celebrate the occasion with prayer and praise, and with personally meaningful ritual. In terms of the human cycle, it could be associated with birth and new beginnings.

Waxing moon

A week later, following the new crescent, the moon is halfway towards fullness. It becomes gradually wider every night, as though it is gaining strength and energy, and is visible for more of the night.

The moon during its growing or waxing phase is associated with our own periods of increase, of gaining strength or momentum, of building up and natural growth. It is a positive, hopeful time, but it requires patience – nothing can be rushed. It can be linked to the human stage of childhood and youth, and to phases of development and learning, the increase of knowledge and understanding as well as physical strength.

Full moon

A fortnight after the new moon, the moon is at its fullest. It is a sphere about the same size in appearance as the sun, rising in the east as the sun sets and appearing to sail across the sky in the sun's tracks, to set as the sun comes up the following day. This, again, is an ancient sign for gathering together for feasting or ceremony.

The full moon expresses maturity, full strength, potency and completeness, and can represent our own times of strength. But the moon has no light of its own: it is a ball of rock that reflects the light of the sun, and it can speak to us at a deeper level of the paradox of spiritual fulfilment as self-emptying in order to be illuminated by God's light rather than our own. When we truly 'shine' with our full potential, is it really our own brilliance, or is it the Divine working through us or reflected in us?

Waning moon

The full moon gradually loses its shape and seems to diminish. It speaks to us of the ebbing away of energy, of decrease or withdrawal, reflecting times of our life when we may feel we are losing strength; things are slipping away or need to close down. This may be a physical experience or a time of life as we approach our senior years, but it can also describe an emotional or spiritual state. A relationship may be reaching an end, a project may be reaching completion, we may be shedding outmoded ideas or perhaps feel less sure, less clear about things, or just less inclined to commit the energy that we have been expending.

Dark moon or absent moon

When the moon is not visible at all, this is often known as the time of the dark moon, although – a little confusingly – it is sometimes also called the new moon.

The 'dark' phase may last for two or three nights, during which time the moon is not hiding. It is simply not in the night sky at all; it is in the sky during the daytime but cannot be seen. The time of the absent moon suggests separation, lack, loss, ending or death, distance, the feeling of having missed something or somebody. It is not a permanent absence; the moon always returns, as it has been doing since before there was life on earth. This can reflect the times in our lives when we know something or someone is missing – most notably love itself, a loved one, or a sense of the divine presence.

Feeling the absence of God is something that many people of faith experience at times in their spiritual journey. It is a feeling. Scripture offers reassurance that the reality is that God never leaves us or stops loving us (Romans 8:35-39), even though at times it might not seem like this. Mystics have described how the feeling of God's absence is a natural part of the relationship between the human soul and God, as the soul's love grows in intensity and longing which eventually is satisfied. A taste of this joy is celebrated with the appearance of the new moon again, and some use the time before its appearance for soul searching and forgiveness seeking, ready for the renewal of relationship.

Journaling

Before moving on, take time to reflect on the way the moon's cycle can speak to our own phases and feelings, and where, if anywhere, you find resonance in your own life journey.

To engage more deeply, look out for the moon and take notice of her cycle, remembering that biblically, both new and full moon are signs for people to gather together in celebration and worship.

A prayer

Holy Trinity of Love,
watch over the changes of our lives,
the times of newness and the times of strength,
the times of diminishing and the times of weakness,
the times when we feel alone,
and when we need to be alone to rest.
Holy Trinity of Love,
Blessed Trinity of Peace,
Gracious Trinity of Mercy,
watch over us with tenderness,
watch over us with kindly light,
watch over us even in the darkest nights,
your presence constant,
your presence glowing deep within our hearts.
Amen

Journaling example

I have always been quite wary of the moon. I thought it was to do with Paganism so I was a bit afraid. But it has helped me to think about how the moon goes around the earth, and how mysterious it must seem to someone who doesn't know about these things; it's added to my sense of wonder at God's world now I know more about it. I can really relate to the phases of the moon. As soon as I heard about the 'absent moon' time I thought of what I had been taught before, about spiritual desolation. It can seem like that – impossible to get that connection with God, and everything seems hollow and pointless. It's a difficult place and difficult to describe to someone with a faith who has never experienced it. I felt I was being judged as losing my faith when I tried to describe it to someone once, but it's not that. I still loved God. Now I can see it as a phase, something natural that will pass.

Chapter 12

The solar year and its relationship with the liturgical year

The solar year is of great importance to the Church. As we have seen – for example, in the commitment of St Brendan to a cycle of prayer that carried him through the years as he journeyed at sea – it anchors the Christian calendar. Whatever is going on in our personal lives, it helps us to identify and engage with the great story of Christ which undergirds the lives of all the faithful. Below, I have described the key elements in this interweaving. Clearly the relationship has a northern hemisphere bias, since this is where Christianity first developed, so for readers living in the southern hemisphere, some translation has to be made. The difference in experience is an insight well worth bringing to the contemporary experience of Celtic Christianity – please do write about this in your journal!

Summer solstice and St John the Baptist

The sun is at full strength, rising to its highest point, the days longest, the nights shortest. It is a natural time to gather for a summer camp with trading and games, feasting and solemnities, and to spend a night of revelry or ritual – or both. The Church placed the celebration of John the Baptist's birth just days after the summer solstice (in the northern hemisphere). John is seen as the forerunner of Jesus, preparing the way for him and baptising him. The summer solstice relates well to the highest point on the circle of the Celtic cross – the number 12 position on the clock.

Winter solstice and Christmas

Six months later, the sun is at its weakest, the days shortest and nights longest. This is a natural time of year for gathering together around a fire to keep warm and generate some good cheer with companions. After this dip into darkness, the light gradually gains strength again. Just days after the solstice, the Christian calendar has placed Christmas, the birth of the Christ-light into the world, synchronised with the renewal of the sun.

The winter solstice and Christmas relate to the six o'clock position on the circle, the downward, earth-pointing aspect of the cross, appropriate for the season in which the incarnation is celebrated: the birth of God on earth, in the flesh.

Twice a year, midway between the solstices, there is a point at which day and night are of equal length. These are known as the equinoxes. Interestingly, the Venerable Bede calculated the most accurate dating of the equinoxes, for his day. The Church placed two angels at these halfway points, which shine like guardians of the two halves of the year.

Autumn equinox and the Archangel Michael

This falls between the summer and winter solstices, around 22 September. This is a natural time for celebrating the abundance of produce that has been gathered or is still being gathered, and for thinking ahead to the winter, making sure that food is properly prepared and stored, or committed for sowing the next year's crops. There is a balance between labour and rest, celebration of blessings and awareness of harder times to come.

Days after the equinox, the Church has placed the celebration of St Michael the Archangel, arguably the most important angel in the Celtic Christian tradition for his role in guarding and guiding souls at night as people sleep and in their final sleep of death, as they make their journey to God. He is a strong warrior of protection and might be seen to preside over the half of the year that moves from summer into winter – the journey into darkness.

On the 'clock' of the Celtic cross, the autumn equinox would be at three o'clock.

Spring equinox and the Archangel Gabriel

Halfway between the winter and summer solstices is the spring equinox, falling around 22 March. This is a time when spring is definitely in progress, the daylight is lengthening and the warmth is gradually returning; new life is all around. It is this lengthening of days which gives us the word 'Lent', a solemn period of abstinence in the Church year, in preparation for what in English is called 'Easter'. Easter is something of an anomaly as the date is moveable, worked out from the lunar cycle and relating to the Jewish festival of Passover. The word 'Easter' comes from the older 'Oestre', a clear derivation from the oestrogen of eggs – the celebration of new life. There may have been a Celtic goddess of the same name. In other countries the Christian festival name is more similar to the Jewish Passover.

The correspondence between the equinox and the Christian calendar is the feast of the Annunciation, in which the Archangel Gabriel visits Mary and tells her she will conceive and bear a son. Tidily, this is, of course, nine months before Christmas. Thus we have Gabriel, whose name means 'God's strength' or 'God is my strength', appearing like a guardian of the growing half of the year.

On the 'clock' of the Celtic cross, the spring equinox would be placed at nine o'clock.

Between these four major events of the solar and Christian year, there are four cross quarter days.

Between the winter solstice/Christmas and the spring equinox/the Annunciation is a day at the start of February. In Europe, this is a natural time to celebrate the birthing of lambs and the flow of ewes' milk, the early days of spring. The lambing festival is called Imbolc, and at this time the highly influential Celtic saint Brigid is also honoured. She is associated with dairy farming and midwifery, as well as with fire and a great spirit of generosity. The Church placed Candlemas at this time, the celebration of the holy family bringing Jesus to the temple in Jerusalem, 40 days after Christmas. It is a time of blessing new birth.

Between the spring equinox and the summer solstice is a time of warming days, beautiful tree blossom, nesting birds . . . vibrancy and fertility. In the pastoral communities of northern Europe, livestock were smoked by walking between bonfires, to rid them of infestations. They were then sent up to the summer pastures, their herders accompanying them, to enjoy a wild camp in the fresh air after months of the cold, damp fustiness of the homestead. This celebration is commonly known as Beltane. The Ascension of Jesus into heaven, the coming of the Holy Spirit at Pentecost and the celebration of Trinity Sunday all occur around this time, but they are tied to the date of Easter rather than the solar cycle. Although it is often overlooked today, the main Rogation day falls in the last week of April. It is a day of appealing to God for protection, and for procession around the fields.

Latterly, in Roman Catholic circles, May has become a month sacred to Mary the mother of Jesus, which perhaps resonates with an older association with the importance of the feminine at this time.

Between the summer solstice and the autumn equinox is the time for traditional European agricultural communities to start the grain harvest, the most significant of all the harvests for a people whose staple diet is bread. This was highly labour intensive, and the success of the harvest would have an impact on people's well-being for the year ahead. It was natural for those who would be working together to gather and enjoy some summertime merriment, and to open the harvest and bless it. Traditionally in some areas there were fairs, races and games around this time. The Celtic Church sanctified the first loaf made from the first of the cut grain, in a Eucharistic service – the loaf mass or lammas of Lammastide.

Between the autumn equinox and the winter solstice, as the days are rapidly shortening and the weather in the northern hemisphere becomes increasingly inhospitable, we come to a naturally mysterious time, the closing down of the old year in a time of misty ambiguity. This was a traditional time of 'thinness' when it was – or is – felt that the spirits of the departed drew close and the veil between the worlds drew back. It was a time of confusion, role reversal, mischief and due respect in honouring the dead. The Church came to place All Saints' Day and All Souls' Day at this time – the ancient Samhain – to pray for the spiritual community, close but beyond us. Soon after this comes Advent, the beginning of the new Church year. Advent in the Celtic Church begins earlier than in the Roman Church, in mid November.

Journaling

- How did you feel about the general sense of interweaving between the Church year and the solar year?

- Did you find yourself warming to particular descriptions?

In the last century there have been highly creative developments in restoring and refreshing the eight solar festivals of the year, and these form the backbone of spiritual practice for many seeking an earth-centred spirituality. For this reason it has become a natural meeting point for many – Christian and non-Christian – who seek to live in a way that is more in tune with the natural processes of the earth. You might have an opinion and/or experience concerning this – for example, through a Forest Church meeting. Have a look at the journaling examples below and consider your own response to the different perspectives.

To review the whole chapter, go back to the questions at the beginning and ask yourself whether there is anything you wish to change or add to your responses, concerning your perspective.

A prayer

In every season I praise you,
O Source of All, O God of life;
I join my song to the chorus of creation,
O Chief of Chiefs, O Lover of all.
Amen

Journaling examples

I love the idea that there are two angels guarding the two halves of the year. Angels fascinate me. I'm wondering whether others like Raphael might have a place in the calendar – I might do some research! It seems to hold the whole year together; suddenly I saw the movement from the dark half to the light half as a great flowing orb, all held in love. I have been following the eight-fold year with my local Forest Church group and we have been using it to help us connect more with the natural world, by noticing what our environment is like at that time and creating Christ-centred ritual that reflects the season. It's a beautiful way of stepping into worship of the Creator – through creation. It's reawakened my sense of spirituality.

Or

We do not really take much notice of the seasons in my church but tend to go with whatever people bring to worship week by week, responding in the Spirit to immediate issues. I've always loved the account of Pentecost and the rushing fire-wind. And, of course, Easter is what it's all about, but we celebrate the risen Lord every Sunday! I wrote some things about Paganism just now but scrubbed them out because looking back, if I'm honest, I thought they sounded quite hostile and I didn't like my own voice. I don't really know much about modern 'earth spiritualities', so I'm speaking from ignorance and I don't want to do that in this journal. I know

I've been brought up to be suspicious of Paganism, but I've got so far on this course, deciding on my own perspectives, that I actually want to go and look into this and find out what I think for myself. I don't see why I should be afraid – 'perfect love casts out fear', and Christ is always with me. I can ask God to teach me and I can ask friends to pray for me. How is talking to Pagans different from talking to neighbours of different faiths?

Or

I have lived within the cycle of the liturgical year for a long time. I go through phases of cherishing the simple continuity, letting it carry me through my days, and then becoming a little weary of the monotony of repeating the same liturgies year in, year out. This has been part of my long spiritual journey – the struggle with impatience and boredom, the self-discipline of staying with the process until I rediscover the joy – which I always do in the end. I was aware of a number of the correlations between the Church year and the solar cycle, but I've enjoyed the challenge of delving a little deeper. By doing so I have found an enrichment to my practice, for which I am grateful. In particular, I relish the reminder about Lammastide, which brings back memories of a rural parish which I visited some time ago, where the little church was strewn with straw and herbs for the blessing of the first loaf in a beautiful enactment of the Eucharist.

Meditation on daily routine

The Celtic cross can help us to form a pattern of prayer as we go about our daily routine. To conclude this chapter, consider the familiar and natural pattern of rising in the morning, pausing to eat in the middle of the day, winding down in the evening and going to sleep at night. Imagine the circle of the Celtic cross taking you through these times. If your routine is different to this and means you are often working at night, the cross can still represent your cycle of rising, working, resting and sleeping, but you might want to adapt the meditation a little.

The first arm of the cross represents waking and beginning the day. This is a moment to pause and dedicate the day to God.

The circle carries you through your morning activity until midday or thereabouts, and the upright arm of the cross. This is a moment to pause and ask for strength or whatever you need for the time ahead.

The circle carries you through the afternoon, until evening and the third arm of the cross. This is a time to pause and reflect, to find things to be glad about and things that have caused concern.

The circle carries you through the evening, until bedtime and the downwards-pointing arm of the cross. This is a time to pause again, and to ask for peace in order to sleep well and to rise refreshed.

A prayer

O Brightest Sun of infinite seasons,
leading us all on our journeys
with your great arc of light;

like the green trees,
so we grow towards you;
like the birds of the dawn song,
so we delight in you;
like watchers in the night,
so we long for you;
the warmth and the life
and the glory of our days.
Amen.

Part 5
What have we done?

Chapter 13
The Celtic cross, the elements and human impact

We can see the Celtic cross as describing the advance of humanity, spreading out over the four directions of the world circle, from our starting point and common ancestry at the centre – whether this is the biblical image of the garden of Eden or, in evolutionary terms, our origin in Africa.

Imagine standing on one of the arms of the cross and looking inwards towards the centre: imagine looking back over human history, the great struggle, the achievements and disasters, as they seem from your perspective. Consider, too, that other people in different contexts have a very different perspective on the history of humanity. Looking towards the centre, the beginning, we also face our own beliefs about creation and the place of humanity in creation.

What do you see? How did this all begin? Did God create humanity to be above the rest of creation, or part of it? Are we born sinful, fallen or inherently good? How far out from the centre have we come, and how much further is there to go? Where are we heading?

Journaling

Pause to consider the questions raised above, and your own thoughts on the rise of humanity, life and creation itself. If you have unanswered questions and concerns, write these down too – you may want to address them at a later date.

Human activity and the Celtic cross: a reflection

An obvious factor that distinguishes us from other creatures is our immense capacity for purposeful creation – and destruction. Yes, bees build hives and birds build nests; moles dig tunnels and beavers make dams; but no creature makes and breaks things as prolifically as we do. Our activity is changing the earth. The Celtic cross can offer us a way of reflecting on our activity.

Find a Celtic cross, preferably one you can hold or touch. Think about the four arms.

Let the long pillar that sinks down to the ground represent the raw resources we obtain from the earth and the process of extracting them – like a drilling rig or a mineshaft plunging into the earth. Let this pillar represent metals, stones, oil and coal from under the ground, clay, sand and timber.

Let the three arms represent forms of energy.

The first of the two outstretched arms represents the force of the wind. Imagine windmills and sailing boats, pollen and seeds carried on the wind. Imagine birds using thermals to glide, kites, hang-gliders, tornadoes and the wind-erosion of rocks.

The second of the two outstretched arms represents water. Imagine waterwheels and hydraulics, wave power, mushrooms pushing through tarmac, coracles floating downstream, rivers carving out channels in rock, floods and bubbling springs.

Let the upward-pointing arm represent the power of the sun, through solar power and through combustion – fire. Think of sun-baked bricks, solar panels, and lizards basking in the sun; think of a campfire, or a lightning strike.

All of these forms of energy exist naturally, and humanity has made use of them since early days. Pause to reflect on the four arms.

Now think about the circle of the Celtic cross. Imagine the circle as a wheel turning. Think of vehicle wheels, machine wheels, cogs, from the tiny mechanics of an analogue watch to the mighty steam engines of times past. Notice the precision, the ingenuity.

Notice how you feel about these different features of the cross. Even if you do not normally 'do' art, consider planning a creative piece to represent earth, air, fire and water in the four arms, and the wheel of human industry. If you were to paint, weave or draw this cross, what kind of colours would you use and what would dominate?

Journaling

• How do you feel about human progress and productivity? What does your artwork say to you?

To balance your work of creativity, take time for a little research, or to collate information you already know. Lots of questions are listed below. Read over them, and notice which ones you feel drawn to respond to.

• Concerning human activity at present, in Western society, where are most resources gathered from, and who gathers them? What are the conditions like for the workers? What impact does the gathering have on the earth? What are the ethical implications of all this?

• How do/did other societies around the world and through history approach industry?

- What are your thoughts on fossil fuels and alternative forms of energy production?

- In our representation of the Celtic cross, how could we represent the by-products of industry, the waste?

- What are your thoughts on the balance between making things that improve the quality of our lives and making things that result in damage to the environment – or to the quality of other people's lives, including people in the future?

- If you see imbalances or opportunities for change in your own life, what are they?

A final question:

- We have reflected on the Celtic cross as a representation of the interplay between energy, natural resources and human activity. Where, to you, is God in all this?

Journaling examples

I find factories ugly, and technology unappealing. We were forever studying the Industrial Revolution at school – it was incredibly depressing. I know people need to work, but I wish there could be greener, quieter, less grimy places for people to work in. I travel by train a lot and look down over warehouse and factory roofs – great grey expanses of corrugated metal and asphalt sheeting – and I dream of them being covered in solar panels and turf, fish ponds, little orchard gardens . . .

I sketched a cross and noticed how hard I was pressing with the pencil, as though I was angry. I drew a massive lower beam, drilled into the earth, and it carried on upwards to form the upwards-pointing arm. It worked well that this one was for fire – it turned into a chimney with smoke coming out of it. What I had drawn looked like a tall factory chimney emerging out of the ground. I remembered how smoke used to be a way of sending messages to the gods, by reaching the heavens. Now, the message, if there is one, is, 'We are the gods.' I wrote this in the clouds. It started to look prophetic, like a tower of Babel about to be destroyed.

The circle came next, an oily smudge coming from inside the chimney, and spiralling out, a sooty, swirling cloud like choking smog. I could feel all my dislike of those history lessons spilling out.

I didn't know what to do with the side arms at first. One became a windmill sticking out from the side, like a TV aerial attached to a house chimney. It was a child's windmill, the energy not going anywhere. For the other side, I was resisting the idea of the Noah story and a huge flood to wipe everything clean. I didn't want to draw that, although this expressed my anger. In the end I drew a canal that people had made, which was the first step in the Industrial Revolution. I drew trees along the bank and fish in the water, because now the canal is used for leisure.

I started to draw ivy growing around the big chimney, and birds nesting in cracks. I think that's where God is, for me. God is nature reclaiming its resources and re-greening. I worried that I should be more human-centric than this, but that is the truth of what I felt. I don't hate our society; I'm really grateful for my own standard of living, but it really bothers me that it's on the back of so much thoughtless destruction. Maybe I feel guilt. Looking at the picture, there are a lot of disturbed feelings here that I could do with processing, I might take the picture to my next spiritual direction session.

Or

I love machinery. I can stand and watch a beam engine or an old sewing machine or a car engine for ages. I love museums of factories where they get looms working, the way one mechanism links to another, the brilliance of the design. Microtechnology is full of wonder, too, but it doesn't hold the same appeal as the iron and steel of days gone by, when people designed things to look beautiful as well as to do the job. We needed progress; our lives are so much more comfortable now than even 50 years ago; people can live longer, and be healthier.

Our technological advances are a real blessing, and now other peoples around the world have a right to develop their standards of living to match ours. We should help them, especially the peoples who live in the lands we took so many resources from. I do think humans matter the most to God, and that the earth and everything on it is for us to use. It does say that in Genesis. I'm not very sentimental about animals and pretty scenery, although I do enjoy them. My concern is more that we might run out of resources because of mismanagement, and be judged for selfishness and greed and a refusal to look at the future. If something causes long-term damage, it's no good. If it's true that burning fossil fuels is raising the earth's temperature and putting people's lives at risk, then it is common sense to plant huge forests and to get designers working on green solutions. God gives us intelligence and inspiration, like the craft workers who made the tabernacle in the desert.

I do believe we could create solutions that support all humanity, and make the earth's resources last indefinitely if we tried. People talk about colonising Mars or the moon – but why not work with what we've got? Why not work out how to make the Sahara habitable? Why not work on desalination; why not put more effort into recycling? God loves us. If we ask, God will help us find a better way of living together for a long time to come. I want to get on with this and make it reality, because I live in the hope that Christ will come back, and when he does, I want him to see how we have turned the world around and started taking some responsibility. How else do we love our neighbours around the world, if we are not concerned about their future and the future of our children? I feel quite inspired to get with a group and do something proactive.

A city walk

Plan some time to walk or wheel around a city, whether you like cities or not. Use the time to notice your feelings and forms of 'elemental' energy, natural resources and evidence of human creativity.

Where is there water? What is your experience of air and sky? Where do shadows fall and sun shine? Where are the cold, draughty streets? Where are the 'deserts'? What natural resources can you find? Look at stone paving slabs and eroding stone buildings, iron railings, marble pillars, timber, gravel. Where are the trees and patches of greenery? What colour are the bricks? Do they reflect the local type of sand or clay, mainly redbrick or grey? What is the human story here? What labour has gone into construction and perhaps defence of the city? Who works on construction and maintenance now? What machinery and resources do they use?

Notice the value judgements you make. Notice your different emotions.

Here is a choice of prayers to use as you go about the city, if you wish – or use one from a different source.

City of refuge you are to me, O God.
Strong rock you are
and place of safety, place of grace.
River of life you are to me, O God,
flowing out from the heart of the city;
a fountain of wisdom you are, a delight to the eye.
City of peace you are, to me, O God,
and peace I pray on this place,
peace in the streets and peace in the marketplaces,
peace in the hearts of all who go their way today.
City of love you are to me, O God,
the centre of all goodness, the meeting of minds,
the community of the holy ones,
the community of those who are touched by love, O God,
the community of those who are living in love.
Amen

Christ of love, encircle me with love,
and so let me find love and let me give love
wherever I go.
Spirit of peace, encircle me with peace,
and so let me find peace and let me give peace
wherever I go.
God of hope, encircle me with hope,
and so let me find hope and let me give hope
wherever I go.
Let there be love and peace and hope in my heart
and deep in my soul,
O blessed Three, O Holy One.
Amen

Human activity in the countryside

While town and city are perhaps the obvious places to reflect on human progress and industry, the countryside, too – certainly in the case of the British Isles – has been shaped and worked by human hands for a very long time. Artwork through the centuries shows the image of the archetypal labourer, toiling over harvest or ploughing, rock breaking or felling trees, long before the Industrial Revolution drew people into the cities and mills to labour over machines and furnaces. The story of people's move between country and town is the story of social change, the cost and consequence of war and rising population, the drive of progress, the struggles of socialism and of capitalism. Whether we live in the town or the country, most of us now are at least one step removed from the wildwood, marsh and moorland which once covered the land. It is no longer our natural habitat.

An outdoor reflection

Try to find a place in the countryside that you can visit, even if it is just the first fields on the edge of town, at the end of the bus route. Try to look on maps and satellite photos of the area before you go, and look into the history of the area so you know a little about the human activity there. If it is impossible to visit, look for a realistic picture or a photograph of a landscape and find out what you can about the place. Imagine yourself into the scene.

Questions for reflection and journaling

• What evidence do you see of human activity? Hedges, walls and fences? Managed fields? Domestic animals? Agricultural machinery? Burned heather? A plantation of trees? Coppicing?

• Where do people live? How do they get about? Is it possible to manage without a car? Where are the centres of their communities and their shops?

• How far back do the buildings date? And what about the gravestones in the nearest churchyard?

• What is the story of this place? Were there once mills on the river, quarries over the hill, mines in the valley, charcoal burning in the woods, encampments of navvies near the railway bridge or the canal embankment, wartime defences along the coast, an Iron-Age hill fort?

• How do you see the balance of wind, water, earth and air?

• Express your thoughts and observations in your journal.

Journaling example

I found this exercise surprisingly challenging. I am a 'townie', but I love the countryside. I try to get out most weekends, cycling or on the train, or for a walk. I chose where I live because it's easy to do that. I find the space and the greenery incredibly uplifting. Part of me would love to come and live in one of the villages I sometimes cycle through: they're absolutely idyllic. I couldn't afford it, and I do feel some envy for the people who can, but I also feel quite judgemental about how much commuting people do, who live in the country and work somewhere else.

I decided to focus on this village and its surroundings. I had never gone into the graveyard, and when I did, I found a surprise: a memorial to the railway workers who died here building the railway that passes through. I sometimes use that line to get here. I hadn't thought about who laid the tracks in the first place, and who blasted the rocks and toiled to cut through the hillside. People died; it was dangerous, difficult work. Here they are laid to rest; they were poor; they were, I suppose, expendable to the industry. Where I have always felt the energy of the wind, rain and sun, the peace now hides a fiery past, like a dragon in the valley. There's some poetry or a song to be written about this; I'm mulling it over.

Work of human hands

One of the largest collections of authentic 'Celtic' prayers is the *Carmina Gadelica,* a collection made by Alexander

Carmichael, who worked in the Hebrides around the time that communities were under immense strain and falling apart because of the advance of 'progress' and the effects of the highland clearances which forced many off their ancestral land. While many of us enjoy the lyricism of these prayers, evocative of a rather special time gone by, they are a memorial of a way of life that was already dying.

Human beings continue to do this to one another. Advances and new ways of managing the land do force change on people – and on creatures, too. The destruction of indigenous ways of life is part of Christendom's history, from the decimation of the peoples who lived in what came to be called the Americas to the stealing of people in Africa to be sold into slavery, and the hunting of aboriginal people in Australia. This is a shameful part of the story of Western civilisation. Colonialism, the imposition of Western values and the hunger for raw materials and land, have made Western countries, with their superior fire power, prosperous. From the perspective of the peoples who were in the way of progress, such interventions have been catastrophic.

The cross as a Christian symbol is one of violence: the execution method of a brutal regime. We meditate on the figure of Jesus suffering and dying on the cross, and we meditate on the empty cross – the joy of resurrection. The cross is a challenging symbol that asks us to look at our own violence. We may go through our whole lives without killing anyone, without harming any creature large enough to notice. But still there is violence, in the very fabric of society, and often we have no idea, or no choice but to condone it. We eat crops grown in countries where people can hardly manage to feed themselves. We use precious metals in our mobile phones and TV screens that we are not even aware of, but for which wars are being fought in other parts of the world. We wear clothes made in factories where conditions are so poor that people's lives are in danger just entering the workplace. The cross asks us to contemplate violence, to confess it, to repent of it. The cross also proclaims the forgiveness of sins, by Christ who died. But the idea of repentance, *metanoia*, involves a commitment to change. The cross ask us to examine our lifestyle and to consider whether we ourselves need to change.

Looking around the world, it can seem difficult to believe that people with financial and military power might change in order to reduce the violence. In this sense, perhaps, the Christian faith marks its followers out as different: there is a different way, an alternative to the 'ways of the world'; a way of justice, peace, wisdom, compassion and equality. How can we live out these values in the beautiful but broken world that is our home?

Journaling

- What does the cross say to you about the violence and injustice of the world ?

- How do you feel about your own potential for violence, intentional or not?

- What do you feel the cross asks of you?

Work of human hands continued

Above, we reflected on the cross. Now we turn to the circle of our daily lives. We considered the *Carmina Gadelica* as a memorial to a dying way of life. Now we will think about how the *Carmina Gadelica* can help us in finding our own prayerfulness as we go about our own routines and journeys. We have reflected on the violence that is a challenging fact of our existence, but now we will reflect on the practicalities of our own personal situation, as we, like people through history, try to do the best we can within our own limitations, aware of our indebtedness to others but hoping to live as well as we can, with integrity.

One of the interesting features of the *Carmina Gadelica* is the quantity of prayers concerning working life. There are plenty of examples of these prayers being reapplied today, in some cases perhaps a little nostalgically: not so many of us have need of prayers while milking the cows, on perilous fishing missions, weaving fabric for our family's garments, or even 'smooring' the fire – carefully preparing the embers at night so that the fire can be relit from them in the morning. It is not so much the activities that are transferable as the attitude of being frequently or continuously mindful of God. It seems that there were prayers and holy songs for everything. Protestant sources refer largely to God alone, as the Holy Trinity, while those following the Roman Catholic tradition include frequent reference to Mary and many of the saints and angels.

Here are some examples of themes for prayer:

- waking up
- going to sleep
- setting out for the workplace
- dedicating a traveller to God's care
- blessing work tools

- blessing the focus of work
- praying for the intended recipients of the work
- giving thanks for domestic animals and what they give
- thanksgiving for and blessing of food
- spiritual companionship of the 'saints' during work
- spiritual companionship of the saints during hardship, such as illness
- prayers of protection for self or loved ones
- prayers for justice and mercy when setting off to court or dealing with an oppressor
- prayers for the newborn, sick and dying.

Here are some prayers which are inspired by prayers from the *Carmina Gadelica*, but using contemporary language and themes. There are plenty of other such collections of prayers by other authors, if you prefer, or consider writing your own. The text of the *Carmina Gadelica* is in the Public Domain and can be found online.[8]

---

8. http://sacred-texts.com/neu/celt/cg.htm (accessed 20 November 2014).

O God, kindle in my heart within
a flame of love for my neighbour,
a flame of love for my friend, for my dear ones
and for those for whom I feel no love
and need your help in prayer.
O God, kindle in my heart within
a perpetual flame of love
that no anger, no bitterness, no struggle,
no grief may put out,
from the smallest to the greatest pain,
with the Holy Spirit to shield my flame
and Christ to tend it and let it grow.
Amen

May the Holy Three
be a guard at my door,
a mantle over my roof,
a rock at my foundation,
to watch,
to guard,
to shield,
to heal,
to surround this place
with perfect love,
this evening,
this night,
this morning when we rise,
today and every day,
tonight and every night.
Amen

Come, Mary, and help my labour.
Come, Bridget and be beside me.
Come to my aid, your kind hands to help me,
as sister, as mother, as gentle healer.
Come love, and come Christ,
to be born anew,
each day that I struggle
to bear God in the world.
Amen

I will place my work before you,
O Holy One, O Beauteous One.
I will hold out to you the work of my hands,
the work of my mind,
the work of my heart.
I will hold out to you, O Holy Love,
all that I do
and all that I am.
Amen

Journaling

Think about prayer. What, to you, *is* prayer? Do you like to talk to God about all your thoughts, or do you prefer to sit in silence, knowing that God knows everything on your heart? What do you do if you have very little time? Do you like to have prewritten or memorised prayers to use? How do you interpret Paul's admonition that we should 'pray without ceasing'?

Consider choosing an area of daily life that you could include in your prayers, and how you might do this. If you already have a routine which includes some of these elements, consider how you might expand it. You might want to focus on the day as a whole, on a specific time, or even on a pattern of prayer.[9]

Journaling examples

I am in a rush from the minute I get up. Mornings are stressful and I often don't sleep well either – they are not good times to sit and pray. My day itself is rushed; time-keeping is important; traffic adds to the problem; any extra thing I have to deal with causes massive problems – fetching a parcel from the sorting office, getting to the doctor . . . Prayer is something I do in church on Sunday, when I manage to get there. I walk through the door and give it all to God, in the company of other people doing the same thing. I feel refreshed, ready to go and get on with the rush.

What is prayer? Giving it all to God, I suppose. I want to offer it all to my loving Father. What could I add? The thought of adding anything to my daily schedule sounds stressful; it's already full. I've got a colleague at work who is also very busy, but she really impresses me. She takes time out to pray because she is a Muslim and follows the tradition of praying five times a day. Prayer is part of her day: it interrupts, but she welcomes the interruption. She seems calm, while I seem stressed. I am thinking, I might try to pause and think about God, let God interrupt my

---

9. For further examples of my 'Celtic' prayers for daily activity, see my earlier book, *Wild Goose Chase: exploring the spirituality of everyday life* (Glasgow: Wild Goose Publications, 2006).

day. I'm constantly looking at the time. If I can start to associate God with this, maybe I can train myself to be more aware. I'm thinking of that lovely Celtic blessing, 'Deep peace of the running wave to you.' I want to say that every time I look at the time: ask for peace.

Or

I work in a warehouse. It is not very interesting, it is cold and I have someone over me who is pretty strict about following procedures properly, so it's boring and stressful at the same time. I really like the idea of asking for spiritual companionship while I work. When I looked back at the list of Celtic saints, I imagined St Aidan coming to work with me. He doesn't look down on me, even though I've got a pretty lowly job; he respects me and cares about my working conditions. He is willing to work alongside me and tell me stories of the Gospels while we work. I've been thinking of him quite a lot as I've been working over the last week, and it's cheered me up. I feel less lonely. I felt like he was right behind me, encouraging me to ask for some help buying thermals. I asked, and they said they would order me a set from the catalogue, and for the others too. Prayer? I've just felt more engaged with Jesus this week, more able to feel loved, finding more things to be glad about or enjoy. That seems to be prayerfulness, even if I'm not saying 'Dear God . . .' all the time.

To conclude this chapter, we return to the title of this part: 'What have we done?' It is clear from observations and reflection that we as human beings have done – and continue to do – a great deal of harm to the earth and to other living things, as well as a great deal of good, yet when we try to define the specifics, we find ourselves differing in opinion: what is good and bad? Are there absolutes? Can we be so clear cut in our judgements in such a complex world?

As we form our impressions of human activity, often we begin by judging others, telling others how they should clean up their act, but finish by looking to ourselves. What we notice in our own lifestyles is our starting point for genuine change. The question can become not 'What have I done?' but 'What can I do?' We can move on from dead-end remorse to constructive improvement. Once we start making changes to our own habits, others notice; we find that groups of like-minded people exist, projects grow and, as in the kingdom of heaven, things that began very small grow to impressive proportions that are difficult to ignore.

Journaling

- Regarding your own impact on the earth, what can you do differently that will be an improvement?

- What can you do alone, and what can you do with others?

Closing prayer

O Chief of chiefs and Love of loves,
forgive me the harm I do in my ignorance;
forgive me the harm I do in full knowledge.
O Chief of chiefs and Love of loves,
change my heart and open my mind,
that I may live in the power of your creative Spirit,
that I may live in the power of your renewing Spirit,
that I may live in the power of your gracious Spirit,
and so walk humbly on the earth
and gently with all life,
loving your creation as I love you, O my Creator.
Amen

Chapter 14
Conclusion

When I look at your heavens, the work of your fingers,
the moon and the stars that you have established;
what are human beings that you are mindful of them,
mortals that you care for them?
Yet you have made them a little lower than God,
and crowned them with glory and honour.
You have given them dominion over the works of your hands;
you have put all things under their feet,
all sheep and oxen,
and also the beasts of the field,
the birds of the air, and the fish of the sea,
whatever passes along the paths of the seas.
O Lord, our Sovereign,
how majestic is your name in all the earth!

Psalm 8:3-9

It is time to draw our thoughts together as we come to the close of this journey of spiritual accompaniment. In so doing, I want to recall a paragraph from the introduction, referring to Psalm 139.

I wrote,

> Psalm 139 . . . expresses awe at God's complete knowledge of us and our ways, which is more complete than our knowledge of ourselves.

As we go through life we gradually learn more about ourselves. Although we can see ourselves very critically, and can be influenced by the way we believe other people see us, we also have the potential to look deep within at the bare bones, so to speak. Self-understanding can become a path to self-acceptance and self-forgiveness as we learn to have compassion on ourselves – even as we are assured that God has compassion on us. This can begin a profound journey towards inner peace and healing, and in turn can open up our capacity to try to understand and have compassion on others.

I hope something of that process of self-understanding, self-acceptance and self-forgiveness has been discernible in working through *Search Me and Know Me*. I hope explorations have at least opened up the possibility of, or played a part in the journey towards, inner peace and healing, which can in turn increase our capacity to understand and have compassion on others. The process is, perhaps, one which includes the realisation that we love because we – children of the earth and children of God – are beloved, as we read in 1 John 4:19: 'We love because he first loved us.'

Search Me and Know Me takes us on a significant journey of exploration, and we encounter many aspects of life: the locations we travel through and dwell in, the people we meet, the creatures we share the planet with, the passage of time and our moods and phases of development. In each case, whoever we are and whatever our personal inclinations and perspectives, there have been two important dynamics.

The first is simple: it is the dynamic of choice represented by the crossroads at the heart of the Celtic cross. Our lives are not predetermined; we have free will and the responsibility to develop our insight in order to make wise choices, choices which affect not only ourselves and those close to us but also those to whom we do not feel connected at all. Our behaviour and our words, as individuals and collectively, shape the world.

In the words of Psalm 8 quoted above, the psalmist marvels that we have been given a great deal of power over creation even though we are part of creation ourselves, and the decisions we make from this position of power affect the interrelationship of life on the planet. The fact that many decisions have been made in the past which have caused harm to the natural world is now difficult to ignore, and we above all generations are faced with the need for wise decisions that will promote healing, sustainability and peace.

This relationship between the crossroads and choice, especially with regard to the use and abuse of power, is illustrated by the Christian symbol of the cross on which Christ died. What are the different choices exercised here? What powers are evident? Unwise, unjust, fearful decisions lead, all too often, to the death of the innocent, but before we condemn the perpetrators in the Passion narratives, we need to ask what is our own part in the use and abuse of the power we have been given over others' lives, over innocent creation? It is difficult today to tread as lightly and cause as little harm as we might like.

The second dynamic is perhaps more subtle, and is represented by the circle of the Celtic cross – its centre and circumference. This can represent the fundamental relationship between our experience of the outer world (the outer circle) and of the inner world (the centre). Reflecting on the world 'out there' helps us to gain insight into what is going on deep in our own inner being – the part of us that God sees.

This inner being is the 'real' us, the heart, the soul, the bare bones, however we like to think of it: the essence which for Christians and others is hopefully undying. This is the very centre of the cross, which is also the centre of the circle on the Celtic cross. The outer circle spreads out as an expression of our engagement in the world, the projection of who we really are, into all that we think and say and do.

When we are not true to our inner being, our interaction in the world is likely to have something unconvincing about it, as though out of alignment. We sense (or others do) that there is something dysfunctional, something that stops us feeling at ease, that stops us feeling free to express ourselves with clarity. We may not really know what we think; we are too busy second guessing what the people who matter to us want us to think.

The word 'congruence' is helpful in this context: circles are congruent when they nestle neatly one inside the other like children's stacking cups. It is a word used in the counselling profession to describe how we need to be genuine, how our true self needs to be reflected in our outer demeanour so that we are making no pretence, no show of being anything other than who we really are. As humans, this can be more difficult than it sounds; the process of working out who we really are, what we really think and what we really feel is a long one – as we have explored in this book.

Knowing who we are, and then living true to that identity because of our sense of self-worth, is part of our path to emotional and spiritual well-being. When we are off centre, it is often the faculty in us for decision making, our crossroads, that is displaced. We make decisions not because we are in tune with ourselves and the divine presence at our heart, but because of some stronger pull coming from somewhere 'out there' nearer the edge of the circle – a pull away from our own inner perception of 'truth' and of meaning and of God. Perhaps it is a difficult boss or a bank manager, the leader of a group we belong to or a very persuasive relative. The off-centredness diminishes our sense of autonomy; it denies us our deepest intimacy: to be in relationship with God in a way that makes sense to us, and so to be centred or grounded or congruent or genuine – or at peace with ourselves.

The more we understand of our inner being or our heart, the more we see ourselves as God sees us. Believing in a judgemental, punishing God causes problems at this stage of self-awareness (see my book *Rejoice with me*), but if we can accept that God loves us, then we can begin to appreciate who we are and allow ourselves to express this in the world, whoever we are, in a congruent or genuine way. This can be very liberating; we realise that we are free to believe what we want to believe and think what we want to think, regardless of what we have been told by external authority figures – those influences that knock us out of kilter. This freedom frightens some authority figures, who feel the need to control their flock and keep everyone together and obedient. It frightens some of the flock, too, because there is some comfort in abdicating responsibility and allowing someone else to tell us what to think.

The path to self-understanding, deciding to do the work on ourselves, to locate what really inspires us, what we truly believe deep down, is life's journey. It is a solitary journey even when we are in company, a path only we can walk, although we can have a good deal of support along the way. It requires discipline and a willingness to listen and learn, to seek out teachers who exhibit a genuineness we know we can trust. While there may be an egoistic element to this need for self-understanding and self-development, the quest is not narcissism, which is a dead end. The spirituality of getting in touch with our own core values and inspirations is relational; we are discovering something of God, for the divine presence is deep within, knowing us, watching us from the inside, as Psalm 139 describes. When we spend enough time reflecting on and learning to love what is at our heart, we discover the mystical presence of God who dwells in our heart.

There is a story about God who sees us from within, in the first book of Samuel.

> But the Lord said to Samuel, 'Do not look on his appearance or on the height of his stature, because I have rejected him; for the Lord does not see as mortals see; they look on the outward appearance, but the Lord looks on the heart.'

1 Samuel 16:7

This is from an account in the early days of the kingship in Israel, when Saul, the first king of the Israelites, was struggling to hold on to his kingship and Saul the prophet-seer was told by God to go to Jesse's household and await instruction on which of eight sons should be anointed with oil as the next king. Samuel noticed how impressive these young men looked – from their outward appearance they seemed like kings. But in each case, until they reached the youngest, God said 'No'. God was not looking for height, muscle or good looks; God was looking for an inner quality. The inner quality is what would shine out, in time, and make the chosen son a true king – one might say the greatest of all the Israelite kings. From that day on, it is said (1 Samuel 16:13), the Spirit of God was upon David: he received divine inspiration and guidance in his ways. David was the one, in God's sight, whose inner matched the outer: he had congruence between the centre of his circle and its outer expression in the world. His inner crossroads neatly aligned with the centre of his being; he would be able to make sound decisions – and what is more important in a great leader?

We can, in a way, aspire to be like David, not to achieve positions of worldly power, but simply to reach our own full potential. Our potential in God, to use another analogy which we explored earlier, is to become that tree-like bridge between heaven and earth, to grow straight and tall towards the 'sun', our true light, to stand firm, to let our roots sink deep into the earth and to bear good fruit in the world. Our potential is not simply to know ourselves, but also to give of ourselves for the good of others.

The fruit we give to the world is not something we can make happen, try as we might. Fruit grows naturally, if the tree has the right conditions. If our fruit is of a poor quality, then we look to the soil, we look at the water supply, we inspect the leaves and bark for disease, we look at the availability of light. When we struggle to give out to the world, sometimes it is because we need help, some fresh nourishment, a change of location even. When we judge the fruits of others, we are often looking at their outer presence in the world. It is easy to dismiss somebody because of what we see. But we can also try to see them as we would like to be seen ourselves – as whole beings requiring understanding. Does a person struggle with inadequate roots? Do they suffer from a lack of nourishment, physical, emotional and spiritual? Are they troubled by diseases of body or mind? We do not always know, but from our own self-awareness, we can at least appreciate that outward 'bad fruit' may well be a symptom of a deep malaise within this person's heart and soul.

As we learn about ourselves, we start to realise just how little we know of others. We usually base our impressions largely on how people seem on the outside, what their fruit looks like and what they choose to tell us. The true person, their inner being, is rarely seen by any but God. We may catch a glimmer especially in those with whom we share the most loving, intimate relationships, but who can know us as completely as the One who dwells in our heart? Learning to appreciate our own worth leads us not to a position of self glory, but to humility, as we cannot help but realise the intrinsic worth of all others, too.

> For it was you who formed my inward parts;
> you knit me together in my mother's womb.
> I praise you, for I am fearfully and wonderfully made.
> Wonderful are your works;
> that I know very well.
> My frame was not hidden from you,
> when I was being made in secret,
> intricately woven in the depths of the earth.
> Your eyes beheld my unformed substance.

In your book were written
all the days that were formed for me,
when none of them as yet existed.
How weighty to me are your thoughts, O God!
How vast is the sum of them!
I try to count them – they are more than the sand;
I come to the end – I am still with you.

Psalm 139:13-18

Amen